The Quantum Heist

By; Mustafa Nejem

PROLOGUE

In a realm where quantum entanglement revolutionizes communication, a band of expert thieves schemes an audacious heist for a quantum-encrypted artifact brimming with rumored power. Amidst the labyrinthine world of quantum mechanics and criminal underworld hazards, they face rival factions, high-tech security, and a quest to unveil the artifact's mysteries before it lands in perilous hands. Yet, as they delve deeper, they unearth the artifact's unimaginable potential, triggering a frantic race against time to avert calamity.

CONTENTS

Chapter 1

Intertwined

In a city full of movement and noise, four people go about their lives without knowing that something important is about to happen. Everyone has their own story, their own occupations, their own paths. Little do they know that their destinies will intersect at a key moment.

Aurora is a very smart person and loves to solve puzzles in a kind of laboratory full of keyboard sounds and bright screens that never turn off. She spends her days surrounded by secret codes and hard-to-solve problems. She loves cracking those codes and protecting important information. She immerses herself in this world in which everything is complicated, looking for the most hidden and difficult to understand corners of digital information.

Cipher is like a magician of the digital world, he moves along the paths of the computer and codes as if he were some kind of sorcerer.To him, every wall of protection he encounters is like an exciting game he can't resist, and every code is like a painting he waits to discover. He is so skilled on the computer that he is said to be a legend in computer security, navigating the complicated paths of the internet without any problems.

Shadow is an expert at dodging glances in the middle of the crowd, he glides without anyone noticing, as if he were a cat moving among people. His ability to stay inconspicuous and to take things without anyone noticing is what really defines him. Everything he does is planned very carefully, as if it were a precise dance, and every time he steals something, he does it with astonishing dexterity, as if he were a talented artist at his work.

Ember is like an explorer scientist in his own world within a laboratory full of formulas and strange things. He's immersed in the world of small things, as if he's looking at what no one else can see. He's constantly doing weird tests and finding out things that no one knows. He's trying to understand how the world works from the smallest things that exist, as if he's searching for the limits of what we think is real and discovering things that don't make sense according to the normal laws of how the world works.Their worlds, hitherto separate, are about to converge at an unexpected intersection.In the gloomy alleys and dimly lit corners of the bustling city, an intriguing rumor whispered that ignited the curiosity of those willing to believe in the extraordinary. Voices floated among the street conversations, subtly driven by the mysterious essence surrounding the artifact.

This enigmatic object was said to be imbued with powers that defied the very boundaries of possibility, powers that could only be associated with the elusive laws of quantum physics.Aurora, Cipher, Shadow, and Ember, each with their own particular essence and talent, found their minds magnetized by this rumor that took shape in the clandestine whispers of the city. The idea of an artifact harboring quantum secrets, which defied conventional understanding, was like a magnet for their restless souls.For Aurora, an expert in cryptography, the mystery of the object resonated with her insatiable desire to decipher, to open complex locks and unravel enigmas. The thought of a coded artifact triggered a spark in her mind, as if it were a puzzle about to be solved.

Cipher, the skilled navigator of cyberspace, couldn't help but feel the pull of rumor. To him, every hint about an object with quantum powers was like a tightly woven web of data waiting to be deciphered.

On the streets, Shadow, with his ability to go unnoticed and his knack for subtle movements, was drawn to the idea of this artifact. To him, the stories that surrounded him resonated with a thrilling challenge, a challenge that could test his skills to their limits.

Ember, the explorer of the limits of quantum physics, found in the rumor a promise of fascinating discoveries and unexplained phenomena. The notion of an object charged with powers that defied the established laws of physics was irresistible to his inquiring mind. Thus, in the secret corners of the city, the rumor became a blazing flame of curiosity for these four individuals, each drawn by the promise of a mysterious object, an artifact with unknown powers that stirred their imagination and awakened their thirst for knowledge and adventure. On a particularly ordinary night, where conversations floated like soap bubbles and laughter seemed mechanical, Aurora, Cipher, Shadow, and Ember's paths inadvertently crossed at a city social event.

Among those present, Aurora, with her keen and eager gaze, was dipping into the tide of chatter, searching for something more than trivial words. As she exchanged comments with strangers, her attention drifted to a detail in Cipher's outfit. A peculiar symbol, barely visible, was camouflaged between the folds of her clothes. A flash of recognition lit up her gaze, though she didn't quite understand its meaning, that unknown emblem generated a swirl of questions in her mind.

At the same time, Shadow, ever alert and vigilant, didn't overlook the details. As he glided through the crowd with the elegance of a feline, his keen perception caught something different in Ember's face. As Ember spoke passionately of his experiments, Shadow caught a glimpse of curiosity in his eyes. That flash, barely perceptible, but intriguing, captured his attention. Against the backdrop of the social hubbub, these flashes of recognition did not go unnoticed by the four individuals.

Between the small talk and forced smiles, the seed of intrigue began to germinate. Though none of them were aware of the full meaning of those flashes of recognition, a subtle current of connection was woven into the air, marking a moment of inadvertent convergence that would resonate later in their lives.

This meeting, seemingly insignificant at the time, became the catalyst for a journey that would plunge them into a labyrinth of mysteries and discoveries. The subtle hints about the enigmatic artifact and the mysterious abilities each possessed became the thread that led them down an uncharted path, a journey that would challenge the very foundations of what they thought they knew.

Driven by curiosity and a yearning to understand the enigma, each embarked on this journey not knowing that this path would change their lives in unforeseen ways. Though at first it was only a subtle breeze of intrigue, it would soon turn into a hurricane of unanswered questions, pushing them to explore uncharted terrain and challenge unthinkable boundaries.

The artifact, with its coded secrets and connection to quantum physics, became the beacon that guided them through an ocean of uncertainty. And the unique abilities of Aurora, Cipher, Shadow, and Ember, which in the past had been a part of their daily lives unnoticed, were now revealed as crucial pieces of a larger puzzle.

Not only would this journey unearth secrets about the artifact itself, but it would test the very essence of who they were. The challenges they would face would not only be physical, but also internal, as the journey into the unknown would force them to confront their own perceptions of the world and discover what it truly meant to be a part of something bigger than themselves.

Chapter 2

Rumor of Power

Aurora, Cipher, Shadow, and Ember gather in a discreet location, ready to share the information they've gathered about the enigmatic artifact that's been generating rumors in the city. The atmosphere in the room was almost palpable, nervousness hanging in the air as each of them presented what they had discovered. Aurora, with her focused gaze and meticulous notes, unraveled the theories that swirled around the enigmatic nature of the artifact. Meticulously crafted details on its sheets of paper, sketches, and equations traced a path to the object's possible connection to intricate quantum mechanics. Her words flowed with a cadence that reflected the depth of her research, highlighting how each finding pointed toward the unfathomable intersection between the artifact and the mysteries of quantum physics.Cipher, in his element surrounded by technology, provided data collected from incursions into security systems. Every bit of information was the result of his expertise in the world of codes, revealing details about the alleged location of the artifact.His presentation was an exhibition of computer prowess, unveiling the routes and accesses, pieces of a digital puzzle that pointed to the possible whereabouts of the encoded object.

Shadow, in his reserved but sharp style, shared rumors picked up on the streets. He talked about rival gangs and shadowy factions, hinting at interests around the object that could trigger clashes. His every word resonated with the caution of one who knows how to navigate the darkest webs of the city, bringing to light information that suggested imminent danger if it fell into the wrong hands.Ember, immersed in his world of quantum theories, provided reflections on the possible consequences of manipulating quantum physics without due care. Their explanations were an exercise in precision, a warning map that delineated potential catastrophes if the artifact was misinterpreted or misused.

He spoke with a seriousness that reflected the magnitude of the knowledge he had gained, highlighting how every action in the quantum realm could trigger a reaction with unpredictable consequences. Together, each presentation created a symphony of information that wove a web of clues, risks, and possible outcomes. Their discoveries were scattered pieces of a puzzle that, together, offered a glimpse of the full picture that lay before them, charting a path marked by uncertainty and the urgency of making accurate decisions.

Amid heated discussions and acrimonious debates, the group immersed themselves in an atmosphere of deep reflection on the potential implications of the artifact. Each argument, each point of view, was woven into a whirlwind of ideas as they explored the limits of the unknown. There was an air of urgency, a tension that was palpable in every word spoken, for everyone was aware of the immense power that this mysterious object held.

The reflections became a journey through the fields of speculation and theory, exploring the possible scope and dangers of dominating such an extraordinary power. There was consensus on the need to join forces, to unite their skills and knowledge in order to acquire the artifact, aware that its value and potential were too great to be underestimated or left at the mercy of inappropriate hands.

Aurora, with her analytical and meticulous mind, outlined the possible uses and applications that could be derived from the

artifact. Her words resonated with a caution tinged by the excitement of discovery, posing scenarios of benefit but also of imminent risk if the object fell into the wrong hands.

Cipher, the skilled navigator of the digital world, presented a pragmatic and strategic approach. It explained how the control of such a power could trigger unpredictable repercussions in the digital sphere, opening the door to manipulations and conflicts of unimaginable magnitude.

Shadow, always reserved but perceptive, provided reflections on the ramifications in the streets, how this object could be coveted by dark forces, triggering a spiral of chaos and danger in the real world. Ember, immersed in his quantum theories, offered a view from the angle of physics and its laws, showing how the improper manipulation of the artifact could destabilize reality itself.

Despite their differences and approaches, each voice converged on a crucial point: the pressing need to safeguard the artifact, to prevent it from falling into unprepared or malicious hands. The consensus stood as a beacon at the crossroads of their arguments, pointing the way towards joint action that would be fundamental in defining the future of this powerful and mysterious object.

In a consensus that resonated with an echo of determination, the group made a unanimous decision to combine their unique skills and work collaboratively to achieve their common goal.

Each pledged to bring their best to the table, recognizing that the sum of their skills could be the key to unraveling the mysteries surrounding the artifact.

Aurora, with her prowess in cryptography and meticulous focus on codebreaking, was committed to pushing her skills to the limit. She would immerse herself in complex algorithms and security protections, determined to unravel the secrets that protected the artifact.

Cipher, with his unparalleled skill in the world of hacking and computer security, pledged to bring his expertise to open the digital doors that guarded any trace of the artifact. Every line of code, every firewall, would be a challenge to overcome in their quest to uncover the whereabouts of the encoded object.Shadow, with his prowess in the arts of stealth and stealth, became the shadow that glided through the streets, securing crucial information, recognizing that his ability to go unnoticed would be essential to the success of the mission.Ember, with his deep knowledge of quantum physics and his understanding of the most complex phenomena in the universe, would embark on the analysis of possible scientific challenges that the artifact might present. His understanding of quantum mechanics could be key to navigating any theoretical hurdles that came his way.With this partnership, each committed to supporting and complementing each other's skills. They knew that the road would not

be easy, that finding and securing the artifact would require patience, cunning, and cooperation. But by weaving together their unique skills, they felt prepared to face whatever it took to reach their common goal.

The group cemented their commitment to working as a cohesive team, recognizing that their togetherness would be the key to overcoming any obstacles on the arduous path to the artifact. It was evident that success would depend on their collaboration and timing, merging their unique skills into a perfectly coordinated tapestry.They congregated at a strategic point, and reviewed the meticulously designed action plan, outlining each task precisely and assigning roles based on their individual capabilities.

Aurora, with its acumen for cracking codes and penetrating security defenses, immersed itself in creating encryption maps, charting the digital paths that could lead them to the coveted object.

Immersed in a constant flow of data and code, Cipher focused on infiltrating key systems, dismantling barriers and creating access where there seemed to be none.Shadow, like the skillful shadow that glides through the crowds, set about gathering crucial information, unraveling the threads of rumors and whispers in the streets, looking for any clues about the artifact. Ember, with his mind dedicated to quantum physics, set about anticipating possible scientific challenges that might arise along the way, preparing to face any anomaly or unexpected phenomenon that the artifact might present.

Each had their role, but they understood that the synergy of their efforts would be the key to success. They coordinated their movements, studying the details of the plan and reinforcing their commitment to supporting each other every step of the way toward their common goal.

The team came together at a defining moment, with unwavering determination reflected in every look. With the strategy meticulously laid out, they embarked on their search for the mysterious coded artifact. Aware of the complexity and danger they would face, each step was imbued with a mixture of excitement and tension.

With a sense of shared purpose, they made their way through dark alleys and digital corridors, each relying on the other's skills and support. As they ventured into uncharted territory, they knew that the trials ahead would test not only their individual skills, but also the strength of their collaboration.

Every alley, every corner of the network, presented a new challenge. But the team moved forward with unyielding determination, navigating obstacles and challenges with cunning and precision. Confidence in their abilities and in the group's ability to overcome any adversity became their anchor, keeping them focused even when the path became uncertain and dangerous.

They weren't just looking for a coded object, they were forging an indelible bond between them. Every challenge overcome, every moment of successful collaboration, strengthened their bond and their resolve to achieve their joint goal. Together, they faced the unknown, ready to dive deeper into the mystery around them, unwavering determined to fulfill their mission.

Chapter 3
The Plan Begins
to Take Shape

With the team committed and united in their search for the artifact, the planning of the robbery takes center stage. Aurora, assuming the lead, gathers the group in a safe and unobtrusive space to chart the steps towards obtaining the precious coded object.

Aurora unfolds a meticulously detailed map. Each line and mark on the map represents an essential piece in the puzzle of the search. With precise gestures and palpable security in every word, Aurora strategically traces the path to the presumed whereabouts of the artifact.

Her keen analytical mind allows the plan to take shape with impressive clarity. Not only does she show the way, but she also assigns specific roles to each, playing on the individual strengths of their peers. Cipher, in charge of computer security, would be given the crucial task of circumventing the security systems. Shadow, with his stealth and cunning abilities, would be responsible for physical infiltration into restricted areas.

Ember, with his quantum knowledge, would bring his scientific understanding to overcome potential physics-related obstacles.

Aurora stands as the guiding beacon of the team, fusing details with a sense of panorama, delineating not only the route to the artifact, but also the roles and responsibilities of each. Her ability to handle the details and visualize the big picture becomes apparent, creating a roadmap that seems to seamlessly tie everyone's skills together.

Cipher dives into the digital abyss of the safety net. The blue glow of the screens reflects the concentration in his eyes, as his nimble fingers dance over the keyboard, weaving a complex web of codes and commands.

Security systems are designed as impregnable fortresses, but Cipher challenges them with unwavering confidence. Every firewall is a door that needs to be opened, every alarm a hurdle to be overcome. With calculated patience and unparalleled skill, he finds vulnerabilities in the system, creating hidden paths as if he were tracing a secret path between lines of code.

Time passes in the tense silence of the room, interrupted only by the rhythmic sound of the keys pressed with determination. With each block overcome, a sense of momentary victory is mixed with the constant pressure to move forward. Cipher moves with cunning and dexterity, navigating obstacles with a sharp mind and unwavering determination. Every achievement is a step forward toward the team's shared goal, and every challenge overcome bolsters their confidence to face what's next.

Shadow, moving stealthily through the shadows of the night. He watches from his strategic hideout, studying with keen eyes the guards' patterns, their routines, and the arrangement of the security cameras. Every step, every turn of the head is carefully analyzed, looking for the slightest loophole that can be exploited.

With the skill of an expert in the art of stealth, he moves gracefully, masterfully avoiding any light that might reveal his presence.

For the team, the information gathered by Shadow is pure gold. Details about security arrangements, guard routines, and timing are essential to the success of the mission. His prowess at infiltrating and his cunning at avoiding detection become the pillars of the team's planning, ensuring that every step is as stealthy as a whisper in the night.

Ember immersed in his laboratory, surrounded by equations, models and simulations. His agile and curious mind dives into the mysteries of quantum physics, searching for clues that may reveal the location of the prized artifact. Each theory and each formula is a key piece in this challenging puzzle.

Ember dives into the theory of quantum mechanics, unraveling the intricacies of particle behavior. It discusses how uncertainty and wave-particle duality might affect the location of the artifact. With his analytical mind and ability to visualize possibilities, he generates hypotheses about potential hiding places based on quantum patterns.

It uses simulation models, performs meticulous calculations, and studies complex patterns in search of subtle clues that reveal the precise location of the artifact. Each new hypothesis is a step forward in the search.

His deep understanding of the quirks of the quantum world allows him to weave theories about the possible locations of the artifact. It visualizes how particles might interact in different spaces, deducing where the encoded object might be hidden.

For the team, Ember's approach is crucial. Their deductions and theories are the compass that guides the search. His deep knowledge of quantum physics becomes a beacon of light amidst the complexity, providing valuable direction on the journey to find the artifact.

At this crucial moment, the team becomes a perfectly oiled cog. Each member plays a vital role, as key pieces of an intricate puzzle. They immerse themselves in their assigned roles with unparalleled dedication, knowing that their collaboration is the cornerstone of this company.

Aurora, her eyes scrutinizing the code, unraveling complex layers of information. Her analytical mind is in full swing, searching for clues, cracking codes, and spotting patterns. Each discovery is a pillar in the foundation of the plan.

Beside her, Cipher dives into the net, navigating digital corridors, the subtle sound of keys being pressed marks his Meanwhile, Shadow glides through shadows and lights, observing, calculating, waiting for the right moment. Their ability to go unnoticed and analyze the environment becomes the group's tactical compass.

Ember, immersed in a universe of equations and theories, exploring the physical basis of the artifact's hideout. His lab is a melting pot of calculations and experiments that light the way for the team.

Everyone converges in meetings, exchanging information, sharing ideas, and adjusting strategies. Words flow like rivers, ideas collide and intertwine, perfecting the plan down to the smallest detail.

This joint work becomes the bastion of their success. They anticipate every move along the way, meticulously preparing for potential setbacks. Each knows that their role is vital, and it is that collective consciousness that binds them together, preparing them for any challenge that stands in their way to the encoded artifact.

In the beat of time, the team immerses itself in the laborious construction of its plan. Every minute counts, every move is critical. Meticulousness becomes their mantra, aware that perfect execution depends on every detail.

Cipher unfolds in the cyber world, weaving hidden paths into the fabric of the web. His hacking prowess is transformed into a digital dance, disabling security systems with the mastery of a virtuoso.

Meanwhile, Shadow studies the scenario, memorizing every movement pattern, every changing of the guard. Every detail in the vigilante's routine is crucial to their strategy, their agility and stealth become their best weapon.

Ember, immersed in the world of particles and theories, analyzes every possible corner where the artifact may be hidden. Their calculations and knowledge in quantum physics are the team's compass, guiding their quest towards the encoded target.

Time passes, but his determination remains intact. They immerse themselves in preparation, refining every task, every move, knowing that success depends on perfection in execution. Each one in their role, aware that their work is essential for the joint triumph.

Chapter 4

On the Path of
the Artifact

With the plan meticulously mapped out, the team sets out in search of the long-awaited artifact, following the clues and signs that bring them closer to its whereabouts. However, the path to the coveted item is not without unforeseen obstacles and unexpected challenges.

Between the grey alleys and desolate buildings, the team follows the clues with determination. Every corner of the city whispers secrets to them, but they are not alone in this quest. As they advance, they sense the threat looming around them: rival gangs, hungry for the same coveted treasure, appear in their path. The tension in the air thickens, turning the journey into a race against time, a battle of cunning and speed.

The shadows in the alleys whisper warnings to them, signs that they are not the only ones craving the artifact. The presence of rivals adds an unsettling hue to their mission, like a discordant melody in an already challenging dance.

The competition adds a layer of urgency to every step, infusing adrenaline into your movements and turning the quest into a dance between allies and adversaries. In this scenario, cunning and speed become valuable weapons while the clock ticks relentlessly.Between shadows and silence, the team takes refuge in a safe enclave, whispers of strategy fill the air. In this temporary shelter, surrounded by walls that keep their secrets, they meticulously review the data collected.

Aurora emerges as a leader, deploying her cunning and analytical skills to unravel potential advantages in this dangerous game. Their deductions are a compass in this labyrinth of rivalries. Like a puzzle master, she sifts through every piece of information, looking for a clue, a clue that will give them an edge in the midst of relentless competition.

The air is charged with the energy of strategy. They discuss moves, anticipate ambushes, and outline counterattack plans.

In this strategic meeting, Aurora's mind is a beacon, guiding them into the light amidst the darkness that surrounds them. Her leadership shines through in the way she shreds every piece of data, every clue, building bridges through the labyrinth of uncertainty.

In the bowels of the network, Cipher masterfully dives into the shadowy communication systems of rival gangs. Every security barrier, every layer of encryption is a challenge you face with skill. It glides like a digital ghost, dodging codes and protocols to access coveted information. His fingers fly over the keyboard, triggering a dance of zeros and ones that unveils encrypted messages, locations, and strategies.

Meanwhile, in the alleys and hidden corners, Shadow becomes the echo of the shadows. With keen perception, he scrutinizes every corner, every passageway, like a specter in the gloom. His ability to go unnoticed is an art he masterfully displays as he slips between urban hideaways.

He observes, assesses, looking not only for escape routes, but for alternate routes that can become his ace up his sleeve in the event of an imminent showdown. Every street, every abandoned building is a puzzle you try to solve to ensure a timely escape route for the team.

At the core of the investigation, Ember unfolds his mind like a beacon in the dark. His understanding of quantum physics is not only a resource, but a guide to

understanding the potential challenges. Their theories and studies become beacons in an unknown ocean, illuminating the potential dangers that may arise from the artifact. Between equations and quantum phenomena, he articulates hypothetical scenarios, each more complex than the last. From quantum coherence breakdown to interference effects, Ember sheds light on every possible consequence, giving the team a crucial overview.

With a razor-sharp analytical mind, he anticipates not only the immediate challenges, but the long-term ramifications that could be triggered by inappropriate use of the artifact. Their mental models work like projections of a movie, showing possible outcomes and consequences that could arise from any decision. Their input is not just a warning, but an invaluable tool for the team, providing a detailed perspective and warning about latent dangers.

Tension builds as the team moves forward, each step on this adversity-ridden path seeming more challenging than the last. They run into obstacles that challenge their wits and trials that wear down their resolve. The traps, ingeniously placed, weave their way together, demanding close observation and quick responses. Every corner seems to harbor a new surprise, making their hearts beat with intensity as they navigate each challenge with cunning and precision.

Amid dark alleys and abandoned buildings, they face off against rival gangs with similar agendas. The air is charged with tension, like a storm that threatens to break out at any moment. Direct confrontation becomes a latent possibility in every interaction, challenging the team's strategy and testing its ability to resolve conflicts without compromising its main objective. Each challenge feels like a litmus test, forging an even stronger synergy between team members as they face these trials that threaten to undermine their efforts.

As they face challenges in their search for the artifact, the equipment becomes a finely tuned problem-solving machine. Every obstacle is an opportunity to demonstrate your dexterity, adapt quickly, and stay calm even in the most tense situations.

When circumstances change unexpectedly, they adjust, transforming uncertainty into fertile ground for their ingenuity. The team, like a well-geared clock, coordinates with precision, bringing out their individual skills and complementing each other to overcome any setbacks.

Challenges don't discourage them; rather, they inspire them to work even more unitedly, forging even stronger cohesion. Hardships are seen as tests of their determination and ability to face the unknown. Each solution found along the way reinforces their resolve to preserve the artifact and protect it from falling into hands that could use it for harmful purposes.

Chapter 5

The Robbery

The team, with its target fixed on the coded device, is on the threshold of the long-awaited robbery operation. They have overcome numerous obstacles and now find themselves facing the safety of the place where the object of their desire is kept. However, complications soon set in, challenging his meticulously laid out plan.

The tension in the air becomes palpable when the plan is put into action. Cipher deploys his talents in the world of hacking, delving into security systems with the same confidence and dexterity as always. But this time, they run into an unexpected challenge: a system far more complex and sophisticated than they had anticipated. Every step he takes, every line of code he tries to manipulate, seems to be backed by an unwavering defense.

Frustration is reflected in Cipher's frown as he navigates the ins and outs of security. With each failed attempt, time becomes more precious. The clock ticks relentlessly, adding extra pressure to the situation. Cipher knows that every second counts, every move is crucial, but he also recognizes the importance of staying calm to meet this new challenge with cunning and insight. In the dim light of the periphery, Shadow notices something unusual. Constantly moving shadows catch his attention, subtle but unsettling signs that something is about to happen. Before he can warn his companions, chaos erupts around him. Rival gangs, which had been lurking in the shadows, suddenly emerge, turning the environment into a sudden and unpredictable battlefield. The atmosphere is charged with

a tense energy, clashes erupt in every corner, forcing the team to react instantly. Shadow is embroiled in an unexpected skirmish, his ability to go unnoticed is put to the test as he tries to navigate between the clashes. Every move becomes a dangerous dance between the minions of the rival gangs and his own moves to evade them.

The team disperses momentarily, each facing the onslaught that arises from this unexpected confrontation. Attention is diverted from the main objective, but the determination to resume the original course of the plan burns in each of them. The immediate struggle to survive and stand firm in the midst of the chaos challenges his focus, but his will to move forward and complete the mission remains intact.

Aurora and Ember are at the epicenter of the operation, facing a scenario that differs radically from their forecasts. The location they had meticulously studied turns out to be a more complex puzzle than anticipated. With the clock ticking down, they feel the pressure mounting, the urgency to find the artifact becomes palpable. Faced with this unexpected complication, they deploy their ingenuity to the maximum. Every corner, every potential gap becomes a point of search. They go on a frantic search, going through every secret compartment, inspecting nooks and crannies, hoping to find some clue that will lead them to the coveted artifact.

Time seems to be compressed, tension is felt in the air as each passing minute becomes more critical. Aurora and Ember's gazes meet fleetingly, but their determination is evident in every gesture, in

every movement, as they search tirelessly. Uncertainty becomes an unexpected ally in this race against time and expectations.

The picture gets more complicated and the team is forced to unify efforts. In this chaotic situation, collaboration becomes the anchor that keeps them afloat. Communication becomes the common thread that weaves their actions, each word, gesture or sign acquires an essential value in this synchronized dance.

Coordination is key, a dance of strategies and tactics that adjust and readjust to the rhythm of unexpected challenges. Each member brings their unique vision of the scenario, sharing information in real-time like pieces of a puzzle, stitching together scattered fragments to complete the picture.

In the midst of chaos, they become masters of adaptability, adjusting strategies on the fly. Quick, calculated decisions are made in milliseconds, fueled by mutual trust and tacit understanding between them. Each relies on the other's expertise to stay on track toward the common goal, a symphony of orchestrated moves to circumvent the obstacles that stand in their way. Tension rises as rival gangs become intertwined with their goals. The situation becomes a tense and chaotic battlefield, requiring coordinated strategies and cooperation to the limit. Cipher, like an artist on the net, dives into the intricate safety net in search of strategic exits. His every move is a pulse of cunning, trying to untangle the blockages that have unexpectedly arisen in his path.

Meanwhile, Shadow becomes the master of distraction, diverting opponents' attention with nimble and subtle movements. His every gesture is a dance calculated to keep away those who threaten the team's advancement. It becomes a moving shadow, averting the gaze and sowing confusion among the adversaries.

The pressure becomes palpable in every interaction as the team struggles to stay cohesive amid the chaos. Adversity seems to multiply, each challenge testing their collective resolve and strength. Despite the complexities and moments of uncertainty, a thread of hope persists between them, a firm conviction in their ability to navigate any obstacle.

Chapter 6

Revelations
and Mistrust

The team has managed to secure the prized artifact, but once obtained, internal tensions arise that threaten to undermine the unity that has so far held them together. The initial euphoria of having reached their goal is clouded by the emergence of suspicion and doubt among team members.

The artifact rests in front of them, a coded object that exudes an aura of mystery and power. Each member of the team examines it with meticulous attention, their minds filled with expectation and, at the same time, with a certain uneasiness about the unknown it contains. The diversity of thoughts and opinions begins to emerge, diverging into different perspectives on how to approach its use and destination.

Aurora, with her meticulous gaze, analyzes every detail of the artifact. Her eyes sparkle with caution and respect for the potential she holds. For her, full understanding of the implications and respect for the limits of her power are essential before any attempt at manipulation.

On the other hand, Cipher adopts a bolder and riskier attitude. His confidence in his abilities leads him to want to explore the limits of the artifact without restriction. He sees limitless opportunities, a vast territory to discover and master. For him, the potential of the artifact lies in its ability to expand frontiers, without fear of the unknown.

The tension between these opposing perspectives begins to weave a web of disagreements and arguments within the team. The divergent visions raise unsettling questions about the future and control of a power that they are only beginning to understand. The atmosphere among team members is densified by the clash of ideas and perspectives. Shadow, shrewd and always on the periphery, detects subtle but significant changes in group dynamics.

His keen instinct to read between the lines and pick up on subtleties allows him to intuit the underlying tensions slowly emerging in the team. His gaze, always alert, captures fleeting gestures and exchanges of glances that reveal more than is said. Concern is drawn in his eyes as he watches as differences of opinion begin to crack trust between members. He feels the shadow of doubt creeping between them, a veil of uncertainty that didn't exist before.

Shadow, known for his caution and ability to read between the lines, begins to question the true intentions behind each perspective. Their doubts become a constant concern, fueling an atmosphere of distrust that subtly insinuates itself into the team's interactions. Their concern now is to discern the true intentions of their peers and to preserve the integrity of the common goal. Ember's dilemma unfolds between his scientific passion and the growing tension in the team. On the one hand, his scientific curiosity drives him to explore the vast possibilities that the artifact offers. His analytical mind envisions scenarios of experimentation and scientific advancement that could unravel the mysteries of the encoded object. However, this desire clashes with growing concern about the possible consequences. Ember, always thoughtful and cautious, cannot ignore warnings of prudence in the use of something so powerful and unknown.

As tension between team members intensifies, Ember finds himself at a breaking point, trying to balance his scientific inclinations with the need to maintain team unity. It seeks solutions that advance the understanding of the artifact without undermining the trust and cohesion of the group, aware that the balance between the two spheres is crucial to the success of the mission.

Tensions are heightened as ideological divergences and personal confessions intersect in the team's path.

The discussions, once animated by the common search, now tinged with a bitter tone, fraught with disagreements that wore down the harmony achieved. Differences, previously masked by the enthusiasm of the mission, were now coming to light, creating deep cracks in the bond between them.

The mutual respect that once guided their interactions was overshadowed by suspicious glances and uncertain silences. Each clung to their convictions and motivations, but the fabric that bound them together seemed to be slowly fraying.

Confidence, that cornerstone that had sustained the team, was now faltering. The roots of collaboration that had fueled their previous successes in the risky enterprise of robbery were tottering dangerously, jeopardizing not only the current mission, but also the very essence of the unity that had once defined them.

The shadows of uncertainty hung over the team, fueling doubts and raising uncomfortable questions that crept into every interaction.

The gaze was no longer directed with the same frankness or sustained with the same complicity as before. Now, every gesture, every word, was scrutinized for ulterior motives, a guessing game that sought to decipher the truth behind the masks that now covered the faces that had once been allies.

Uncertainty about the true implications of the artifact echoed in every conversation, a constant echo that eroded the trust built with care. Theories about its use and consequences intersected with suspicions and fears, creating a whirlwind of suspicion among team members.

Chapter 7

The Hidden Power

Ember immerses himself in the study of the artifact, eager to unravel the mysteries it contains. With a meticulous approach and a passion for quantum physics as a guide, he begins to unveil the first layers of secrets surrounding the coded artifact.

The artifact opened before Ember like a book of secrets, its pages revealing a complexity so extraordinary that it defied even the most advanced theories of quantum physics. Each twist, each layer uncovered revealed capabilities that defied all known logic, and each new revelation shot his mind into unknown territories of limitless possibilities.

Ember was immersed in a tangle of discoveries, amazed by the depth and scope of the artifact. What had begun as a quest fraught with uncertainty now became an unprecedented discovery, a vision of a potential that could reshape the fundamental laws of existence itself.Excitement flashed in Ember's eyes, a mixture of awe and excitement reflected in his face, aware that they had unearthed a power that could alter the course of the known universe.

The artifact, in its unfathomable enigma, revealed paradoxes in its very essence. Ember, between fascination and uneasiness, unraveled its darkest secrets. Between the lines of quantum physics, he found uncomfortable omens. As he immersed himself in his notes, he stumbled upon haunting clues, insinuations buried among formulas and equations. Flashes of warning suggested that the power encoded in the artifact was as vast as it was dangerous, capable of unleashing forces that transcended the known laws of the universe. In his enthusiasm for limitless potential, he also found ominous signs, warnings whispered by the very essence of the object that began to weave a web of fear and caution. At the intersection of wonder and awe, Ember finds himself, as if on a precipice, contemplating two sides of the same coin: the artifact, unveiling its fascinating enigmas and ominous warnings. Every revelation, every flash of potential, is amalgamated with an echo of alarm in his mind, an inner voice that insists on the latent danger, a warning that awakens a subtle but persistent unease.

The brilliance of infinite possibilities clashes with the shadows cast by uncertainty. In awe at the capabilities the artifact could offer, a wall of unease also rises, a constant reminder that greatness involves palpable risk. The duality of the artifact is reflected in the duality of emotions that stir within Ember: the wonder of the unknown and the wariness of the unpredictable.At the core of his being, Ember struggles with a throbbing, heart-wrenching dilemma.

Every discovery, every trail of information triggers a storm of mixed emotions. Scientific wonder is intertwined with moral anguish, creating an internal discord that wounds his conviction. Curiosity drives him forward, eager to unravel the secrets of the artifact, but responsibility weighs heavily on his conscience.

The brilliance of the artifact's potentialities clashes with the ominous shadow of its possible risks. Ember becomes embroiled in a whirlwind of ethical dilemmas, caught between a fascination with the unknown and a moral obligation to warn of latent dangers. The desire to explore the revolutionary capabilities of the artifact is intertwined with the need to warn of the imminent risks that could be triggered by negligent manipulation. This inner conflict becomes a mental labyrinth, where paths to exploration collide with warnings of caution and prudence.Among team members, Ember's revelation adds an unexpected dimension to an already tense landscape.

The artifact, once only a coveted goal, now presents itself as an enigma shrouded in uncertainty and risk. Discussions about its fate and the ethical dilemma of its use become an intellectual battleground. Each member of the team defends their point of view, weaving arguments between the need to explore their potential and the duty to safeguard the world from possible catastrophic consequences.

Chapter 8

The Hunt Begins

Obtaining the artifact has not gone unnoticed by rival gangs who crave its power. Efforts to get hold of the encoded object intensify, triggering a series of dangerous encounters between the team and their competitors.

In the shadows of the city, a curtain of mystery unfolds. Team members begin to sense the subtle, yet unsettling, hints of danger that lurks in front of them. The furtive glances, shadows in the alleys, a constant murmur of vigilance perceived at every movement: clear signs that rival gangs are weaving a relentless web of stalking, eager to snatch the artifact.

Every alley, every corner seems to harbor a suspicious shadow, every unfamiliar face evokes a sense of impending danger. The city becomes a chessboard where every move is analyzed, every step watched by invisible eyes. Tension is palpable in the air, a feeling of constant stalking that envelops the team, keeping them on high alert at every moment.

Rival gangs, cunning and hungry for the artifact's power, have unleashed a silent hunt, pursuing its trail with predatory determination. Competition intensifies, turning every corner into a potential arena of confrontation, and every shadow into a latent threat.In the eye of the storm, the team is drawn into a chaotic dance in the shadows of the city. Shadow, his senses sharpened, detects the first signs of impending danger. Rivals, stealthy and determined, draw closer, lurking from the shadows of the alleys.Encounters become inevitable, a clash of interests in an unpredictable scenario. Confrontations erupt in dark corners, between abandoned buildings and deserted streets, where every shadow hides a latent threat. The echo of hurried footsteps and haunting whispers fills the tense air, as tension rises to a boiling point.

The team is forced to act quickly, moving between dodging ambushes and confronting their pursuers in a dangerous dance. Every corner is a potential battlefield, every alley a stage where confrontation becomes inevitable. In the midst of this chase, adrenaline and uncertainty intermingle, fueling the urgency to find an escape route in this labyrinth of threats.

In the midst of the frantic chase, Cipher displays his tactical prowess. With calculated, quick movements, he immerses himself in rivals' communication systems, manipulating information and creating skillfully orchestrated distractions to confuse those who pursue them.

Each ruse designed by Cipher seeks to create chaos among the rivals, diverting them from the team's route and offering them escape loopholes. However, the cunning of their opponents poses constant challenges: every time they manage to dodge a siege, they face new onslaughts, forcing the team to redefine their evasion strategies.

The art of Cipher hacking becomes a digital dance, a choreography of ingenuity and cunning against an enemy whose reach seems limitless. With each maneuver, Cipher tries to gain precious seconds, even if each strategic move only momentarily manages to push away the impending confrontation. Tension builds as the team becomes embroiled in a dangerous game of cat and mouse, where each short-lived victory triggers a new challenge.

In the tense scenario of the chase, the team is immersed in a duel of ingenuity and tactics. Each step becomes a test of skills, with the artifact as the centerpiece on a board where survival and victory are intertwined.

The individual capabilities of each team member are put to the test in a context of extreme adversity. Aurora displays her keen intelligence, analyzing escape routes and alternative strategies to elude her pursuers. Her quick mind and methodical approach become the beacon that guides the group through times of confusion.

Shadow explores hidden routes and creates unexpected exits, defying the logic of the ambushers and taking advantage of every corner as a temporary shelter.

Ember, with his scientific mind, tries to foresee movements and reactions based on quantum physics, trying to anticipate the patterns of rivals and find a way out

The fight to protect the artifact becomes a dangerous, where each individual skill and dexterity combines to challenge adversaries in a race for survival and the fate of the coded object

Aware of the magnitude of the responsibility that rests on his shoulders, he desperately searches for ways to safeguard the artifact. The weight of this burden is felt in every beat of your heart, in every thought that crosses your analytical mind.

Tensions, already palpable in the team, reach a fever pitch. Each strategy of the rivals is a more difficult challenge to overcome than the last, their movements become more calculated and their ambushes more coordinated.

Time seems to be against them, as if they were racing against an invisible clock. Each onslaught leaves a mark on the team's resolve, but it also strengthens their resolve to protect what they've risked so much to achieve. Ember, with his scientific mind always in action, tirelessly searches for strategies to safeguard the artifact as they face the onslaught of rivals.

The pressure is overwhelming, and in the midst of this whirlwind of conflict and challenges, the team clings to the hope of finding a solution that will ensure the safety of the artifact while also their very survival in this ruthless race.

Relentless persecution forces them to unite beyond their internal differences and conflicts. In this fight for survival and protection of the artifact, they cling to a thread of hope, relying on their individual skills and coordination as a team to overcome the onslaught that awaits them.

Chapter 9

Confrontations
and Betrayals

The team, already under constant pressure from rival gangs, is plunged into a whirlwind of betrayals and internal conflicts that shake the foundation of their unit.

In the team's dynamics, Aurora and Cipher have become polar opposites. The prudence and moderation that have always characterized Aurora clash directly with Cipher's boundless ambition. The artifact, a focal point of this tension, acts as a catalyst for their disagreements, creating a rift in their relationship that deepens and deepens.

Aurora, with her thoughtful and cautious approach, sees the artifact as a potential hazard that must be approached with extreme caution. Their stance is to safeguard and study the object meticulously, making sure they understand all the implications before proceeding. However, this prudence clashes with Cipher's attitude, who yearns to unlock the hidden power of the artifact without restriction, leading him to defy Aurora's warnings and considerations.

The discrepancy in their approaches has triggered a conflict of ideals, and the once harmonious relationship is now mired in a battle of opposing perspectives. Every conversation between the two seems to become a minefield of disagreements, echoing their divergent views on the handling and use of the device.

In the depths of his trademark caution, Shadow has begun to notice something murky among the team's ranks. From his watchful and reserved position, he has picked up diffuse but disturbing signals. Faint hints, such as low-toned conversations and fleeting gestures, have aroused his suspicions.

This silent observer, always in the shadows, detects the emergence of divergent interests and masked agendas. His doubts, which were once barely a whisper in his mind, now become persistent and more troubling.

Always calculating and cautious, Shadow doesn't underestimate signs of discord that could undermine team cohesion. As their concern grows, their vigilance task becomes more intense

Eyes meet looks of doubt, in the heart of the storm, an unexpected twist changes the course of the

situation. Carefully guarded secrets come to light, revealing agendas that until then had remained veiled. Trust, the glue that held the team together, cracks like brittle glass when exposed to the light of betrayal.

The foundations of the group are shaken by this revelation. The gazes, once full of complicity, now find themselves in the middle of an abyss of confusion and mistrust.

Every word once shared with sincerity, now feels fraught with doubt. The feeling of betrayal weighs heavily on the shoulders of each team member, sowing the seeds of mistrust and leaving a mark of uncertainty at the core of the group.

Chapter **10**

The Quantum Spin

The team, mired in internal tensions and mistrust, is faced with an unexpected twist when they discover an astonishing ability of the coded artifact: its ability to alter reality itself. This discovery shakes the foundations of their understanding of the world and sets off a series of extraordinary events. In his unwavering quest for knowledge, Ember plunges into a sea of experiments. One of these deeper inquiries reveals a discovery that challenges the very foundations of its understanding. He stumbles upon a singular pattern, a hitherto unknown phenomenon. The artifact, shrouded in mystery, exhibits a surprising ability: it seems to have the power to shape reality itself.

Each test confirms this strange power: subtle, but undeniable alterations in the environment. They manifest as vibrations in the fabric of reality, changes that defy established logic.These discoveries arouse in Ember a mixture of astonishment and apprehension; Wonder at the unknown is mixed with uncertainty about the consequences of such an influence on the world they know.

News of the artifact's potential to alter reality as it is known leaves the team in a state of awe. The magnitude of this discovery is overwhelming, it's as if they've opened the doors to unknown and amazing, but also terrifying, territory.

The news spreads among them like wildfire, unleashing a swirl of contrasting emotions. On the one hand, the amazement and fascination at the idea of something so extraordinary and powerful, something that until then seemed unattainable. On the other hand, fear infiltrates their thoughts, fueled by uncertainty about the possible consequences of such an immense and destabilizing power.

This revelation makes them question the limits of what they thought possible and plunges them into a sea of uncertainty about the future of their own lives.

As Ember deepens his studies, he discovers that the artifact's influence is not limited to the confines of his lab. What seemed to be an exceptional discovery soon unleashes a series of puzzling and incomprehensible events.

Reality begins to twist in unexpected ways. Events that defy any logical explanation begin to happen around him. Natural laws, once so predictable, now falter and wobble, as if the world were dancing to an unknown tune. The perception of reality becomes blurred, and the distinction between what is considered possible and what is impossible blurs in a haze of uncertainty.It is as if the barriers between

the boundaries of the known have been broken, allowing the extraordinary to seep through invisible cracks. Every day becomes a mystery to be solved, every event defying logic and conventional understanding, leading team members into a state of constant perplexity.

The streets, once familiar and predictable, are transformed into scenes of unusual and disconcerting events.The power of the artifact manifests itself in every corner, defying logic and pushing the boundaries of reality to a point that arouses awe and bewilderment in the team.

Events become uncontrollable, a succession of unusual incidents. Objects floating for no apparent reason, distortions in time that make clocks work capriciously, and flashes of light dancing in the night sky. The very nature of things seems to be altered, giving rise to situations that defy all rational explanation.

Disbelief is intertwined with awe as team members try to comprehend the magnitude of what they are witnessing. Each extraordinary event becomes a challenge to their understanding of the world, leading them into a state of constant perplexity as they try to decipher how an artifact can trigger such an alteration in reality.

The team is plunged into an unprecedented dilemma. What was once the object of longings and ambitions now becomes a disorienting enigma. The artifact, once desired for its promise of power, reveals itself to be an uncontrolled force that challenges the foundations of his understanding of the universe. As they struggle to decipher and contain this altered reality, they encounter obstacles that transcend the boundaries of their imagination.

Buildings seem to bend before your eyes, shadows come to life, and the lines between the tangible and the ethereal blur. In this whirlwind of the unpredictable, your understanding of the world teeters on a precipice of uncertainty.

Discussions turn into frenzied debates about how to handle this challenge. Each idea clashes with the next in an effort to find a solution to what seems to be an impossible puzzle to solve.

Chapter 11

The Dissolution
of Reality

In an even more turbulent turn, the artifact's ability to distort reality takes on an unforeseen ferocity. What was once a series of inexplicable phenomena now becomes a dizzying succession of events. The world that the protagonists thought they had understood and mastered becomes a distorted reality, taking them into unknown and bewildered territories.

The very foundations of existence seem to be tottering. Natural laws are blurred, gravity becomes a suggestion rather than a rule. The streets, once familiar and orderly, twist and fold like reflections in a warped mirror. Time vanishes into fragments, creating suspended instants and inexplicable lapses that defy all temporal logic.

The team confronts this whirlwind of distortions with a cocktail of awe and awe. Every step forward is uncertain, every move is shrouded in an atmosphere of unpredictability. Reality becomes a chaotic canvas, where familiar rules vanish and are rewritten around every corner.

Phenomena that were once perceived as isolated anomalies are now multiplying exponentially, twisting the very essence of reality. The streets are transformed into unrecognizable landscapes, fragments of a distorted reality. Gravity becomes capricious, pulling objects in impossible directions, defying known logic.

The buildings seem to twist and melt like ephemeral sculptures on an unstable canvas. Colors and shapes fade and blend into a surreal palette, creating cityscapes that defy visual coherence.

Time, that bastion of linearity, becomes a turbulent river of scattered instants. Moments that should logically follow each other slide over each other, creating a collage of pasts, presents, and futures. The protagonists find themselves trapped in a temporal labyrinth, where the ordered sequence is lost in a whirlwind of disconcerting moments.

This chaos of distortions challenges the perception and understanding of reality. The boundaries between the possible and the impossible blur, taking the protagonists into uncharted territory.

Aurora finds herself in a swirl of contradictory emotions, she used to embrace logic and reason. Each anomaly is a challenge to her meticulous understanding of the world, leaving her mind in a state of perplexity and intrigue.

Cipher, whose computer skills used to provide a sense of control, now faces an unpredictable scenario. Every distortion in reality poses a puzzle beyond its binary comprehension. The fascination with the unexplored is mixed with the restlessness of a territory that cannot be mastered by its conventional skills.

Shadow, normally clinging to the solidity of his instincts, finds himself shrouded in a blanket of uncertainty. The reality that he could once read like an open book now becomes a labyrinth of disconcerting surprises. The mix between his ability to interpret the environment and the avalanche of distortions challenges his view of the world, bringing him to a constant state of alert. Ember faces a reality that defies all known theories. His analytical mind struggles to reconcile inexplicable phenomena with established physical laws, immersing himself in a constant quest to find logic in chaos.

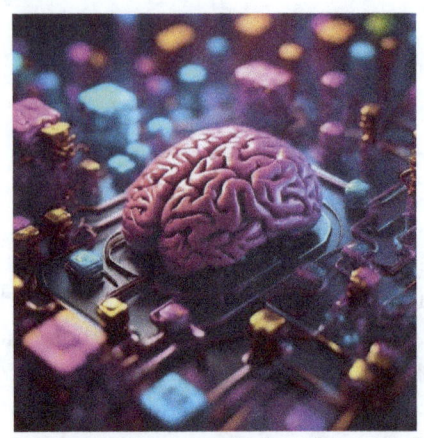

For each of them, wonder and awe coexist, plunging them into uncharted territory where the boundary between possible and impossible vanishes before their very eyes.

At the heart of this bewilderment, the protagonists find themselves in a labyrinth of ignorance. Each attempt to find a logical explanation drags them further into the maelstrom of uncertainty.

Aurora, usually grounded in logic and the scientific method, plunged into an ocean of questions with no clear answers. Every attempt to apply their knowledge vanishes in the face of strange events that defy all known understanding. Confusion and intrigue grow in his analytical mind, each finding questioning what he once regarded as immovable truths.

Cipher, whose skills are based on code certainty and binary logic, finds himself in challenging terrain. Each attempt to decode this mystery only adds layers of complexity, challenging the very foundation of their abilities.

Shadow confronted with a reality that changes in an instant. The uncertainty that surrounds him undermines his ability to anticipate movements, leading him to a state of perpetual alert.

Ember, whose scientific mind is constantly searching for underlying patterns and laws, is confronted with a phenomenon that contradicts all acquired knowledge

Together, are immersed in a world of enigmas that challenge their perceptionn, taking them on a journey through the unknown in search of answers that seem to fade with each step taken.

Amid uncertainty and unease, the team struggles to come to terms with the magnitude of the disruption to their environment. Each member, pushed by the bewildering new reality, plunges into a state of constant restlessness and questioning.

Aurora faces a scenario that challenges the fundamental laws she had studied so much. Every attempt to apply their scientific knowledge is thwarted by the irruption of inexplicable events that undermine their confidence in objective reality.

Cipher, skilled in decoding and understanding complex systems, is overcome by the chaotic and seemingly meaningless nature of the phenomena that are unleashed. Every attempt to find logical patterns in this new reality dissolves through his fingers.

Shadow is faced with a scenario in which shadows seem to take on a life of their own, challenging his ability to anticipate and dodge the dangers hidden among the changing landscape.Ember is confronted with a paradigm that completely escapes the known laws of physics and nature. Every

attempt to find rational explanations only leads to more questions and bewilderment.The foundations of reality are wobbling, challenging their fundamental beliefs and leading them to a crossroads where conventional understanding seems to fade in the face of the unexpected new reality that surrounds them.

Faced with a reality that seems to resist comprehension, the team is immersed in a maelstrom of efforts to restore coherence to the world around them. Every attempt to restore stability seems to challenge them even more, plunging them into a labyrinth of uncertainty and bewilderment.Aurora, with her eagerness to find patterns and meaning in confusion, leads attempts to find logic in chaos. Every theory she formulates dissipates in the face of the overwhelming complexity of events that follow one another in no apparent order.

Cipher, normally precise in his strategies, is overwhelmed by the unpredictability of the situation. Each attempt to decipher the erratic patterns that manifest only seems to lead to more chaos and disorientation.

Shadow, always on the lookout for lurking shadows, finds himself battling a darkness that seems to have a will of its own, preventing him from anticipating or dodging dangers that are unpredictably unleashed.

Ember, looking to science for answers, is challenged by phenomena that defy rational explanation. Each experiment and analysis only throws up more questions, plunging him into a sea of doubt and bewilderment.The team, united by confusion and determination to solve this conundrum, is plunged into a never-ending cycle of failed attempts to restore stability. Each effort seems to trigger further disruptions, leading them into a spiral of bewilderment that defies their comprehension and resistance.

Chapter 12

The Search
for Answers

The team finds themselves caught up in a whirlwind of anomalies, battling a world that twists and distorts before their eyes. In the midst of this frenzy, Ember emerges as a beacon of determination, taking on the challenging task of deciphering the true essence of the artifact.

Ember, in his eagerness to understand, immerses himself in the exhaustive study of the artifact, searching through the veins of his knowledge for any clue that sheds light on the chaotic situation. Their dedication becomes a beacon in the midst of the confusion, while implausible events continue to follow one another without apparent meaning.

Each piece of the artifact is meticulously examined, its possible effects and properties analyzed with scientific zeal. However, as much as Ember immerses himself in science, the altered reality that surrounds them seems to escape any known logic.

Members of the team, place their trust in Ember, yearning for answers that can restore order to a world that seems to have lost its coherence.

As Ember delves deeper into the study of the artifact, his mind becomes a hive of theories and hypotheses, searching for a glimmer of understanding amid the confusion. Every discovery, every small breakthrough, is a glimmer of hope in an overwhelmingly puzzling landscape.

In the lab, he becomes a pillar of relentless dedication, devouring pages of quantum theories and immersing himself in endless experiments. The passion for quantum physics turns into a burning obsession to unravel the enigma surrounding the mysterious artifact.Each formula is meticulously shredded, each equation examined to its ultimate implications. Ember searches for answers in the winding labyrinth of quantum physics, where each discovery becomes a starting point for new conjectures and unexpected challenges.The laboratory becomes a melting pot of activity, replete with devices and apparatus that distill the very essence of science. Ember's mind transforms into a vortex of creativity and focus, each neuron dedicated to unraveling the secret that lies hidden in the artifact.The experiments follow one another relentlessly, each result, whether a breakthrough or a new unknown, prompts Ember to delve even deeper into the core of the mystery. Each new lab test is a step forward, but it's also a constant reminder of the vastness of the unknown that the artifact holds.With each step closer to the truth, Ember dives deeper into the intricacies of the artifact, pushing the search for answers to the edge of the known and challenging the frontiers of scientific understanding. Every failure is a challenge, every success is a light in the midst of the darkness that surrounds the enigmatic object.

The ethical dilemma hangs over the team like an unsettling shadow, obscuring their debates and decisions. Discussions burn with intensity, unraveling the moral complexities surrounding the artifact. Each team member finds themselves caught at an ethical crossroads, debating the pros and cons of using the overwhelming power of the artifact.

The arguments are woven into a tangle of ethical dilemmas. Cipher, with his eagerness for exploration, defends the possibility of harnessing the capabilities of the

artifact to unravel new knowledge and achieve unprecedented progress. In contrast, Aurora warns about the risks of manipulating a power that escapes her comprehension, advocating prudence and caution.

Shadow, the silent observer, casts wary glances and warns of the unknown consequences that could emerge from altering reality. Meanwhile, Ember, immersed in science, faces an internal battle between fascination with the discovery and concern about the unpredictable implications of the artifact.

The discussions become a dance of passionate arguments, each presenting their view of right and moral. The debate evokes fundamental dilemmas about free will, responsibility, and power. Uncertainty about the path forward becomes an emotional and mental obstacle for the team, stirring the waters of trust and cohesion that once held them together.

In the midst of this moral crossroads, Aurora, Cipher, Ember and Shadow find themselves in a harrowing dilemma. Each one contemplates the ethical abyss that opens up before them, questioning the limits of their responsibility and the possible magnitude of the consequences.

Aurora, with her ingrained prudence, struggles to stay true to her initial conviction: control of the artifact could unleash a torrent of uncontrollable chaos. Her voice, full of caution, rises to remind them of the possible disasters that could arise from an improper use of the power possessed by the artifact.

At the other extreme, Cipher, with his unquenchable thirst for knowledge and advancement, advocates exploration and harnessing the artifact's capabilities. His optimistic and ambitious vision of the future clashes directly with Aurora's warnings, arguing that power must be used to understand and shape reality.Shadow, the meticulous observer, is at the center of this moral controversy. His loyalty to the team is undeniable, but his fear of unanticipated consequences causes him to vacillate between opposite extremes. He weighs every word and every argument, aware that any decision could have unpredictable ramifications.

The internal debate becomes a whirlwind of moral and emotional dilemmas that shake the foundations of their convictions. Responsibility and danger, duty and risk, are intertwined in a tangle of uncertainty that clouds their judgments and challenges their most deeply held beliefs. The team finds itself in an ethical abyss, wrestling with a decision that seems to challenge the very foundations of their morality and teamwork.

For Aurora, the voice of caution, responsibility weighs like a slab. Their arguments are submerged in a sea of uncertainties, fears that creep in about the possible lack of control if the power of the artifact is unleashed. The catastrophic vision of what could happen becomes their standard, striving for prudence and security.Cipher embraces the possibility of a new horizon, pushing forward with bold optimism. Exploring the artifact's potential becomes its cause, dazzled by the promises of knowledge and advancement that could arise from its use. His determination defies warnings, seeking opportunity in the unknown.Shadow is caught between these opposing currents. Loyalty to one's peers clashes with the uncertainty of unpredictable consequences. Each option represents a risk that he meticulously measures, fearing the division that any election could generate. Doubts, and the responsibility of making a decision, the magnitude of which could change their destiny and that of the entire world, weigh on each member of the team.Their unity is put to the ultimate test, as they teeter on the brink of a choice that could define their future and that of everything they know.

In the midst of Ember's maelstrom of investigations, the team finds itself caught in an existential dilemma that shakes the foundations of their cohesion.

Hours pass as the group faces an ethical dilemma that weighs heavily on their shoulders. Which way to go? The decision to use the artifact in an attempt to restore reality and, in the process, risk unleashing even greater chaos? Or the alternative of not acting and risking that the current distortions become irreversible?

The clock ticks every second, every tick seems like a heartbeat of urgency. The looks are met in a mixture of worry, fear and determination. Aurora, Cipher, Shadow, and Ember each have their own concerns, facing the doubts and responsibilities that this decision imposes on them.

Aurora, embracing prudence, raises arguments loaded with concern about the repercussions, reminding them the catastrophic potential that the artifact could unleash. Her words are a call for caution and to think about the long-term consequences.

Cipher, defends the possibility of using artifact as a pathway to new frontiers of knowledge.

Shadow, contemplates the pros and cons of each option, worried about the possible consequences of both decisions. Their silence reveals an internal struggle between loyalty, risk, and responsibility.

Ember, feels the weight of responsibility. Every discovery, and every theory formulated brings him closer to understanding the artifact.

The team is on a precipice, at a time when their decisions could trigger a turn in their destiny and that of the entire world. Between the pressure of time and the uncertainty of the unknown, they must find an answer that clears the shadows and guides their path through this whirlwind of ethical dilemmas.

Chapter 13: The Battle for Control

At the epicenter of a crossroads that challenges its integrity, the team is at a breaking point. The pressure of time and the constant threat of adversaries place them in a situation of limit, forcing them to confront imminent decisions. The artifact, coveted by multiple factions lurking, represents both an object of protection and a tool of incredible power.

Rival gangs, on the hunt for the artifact, tighten the siege, their presence becoming more and more palpable, a constant reminde r that time is running out. The team, in the midst of this relentless siege, is faced with an inescapable dilemma: protect the artifact, safeguarding its potential to change the course of reality? Or use their capabilities for their own interests, risking unpredictable consequences?Reflection on these options divides the team, generating heated debates that reflect the discordant voices of its members Aurora, pleads for the protection of the artifact, fearful of the catastrophic consequences that could be unleashed if it falls into the wrong hands. Her voice is a call for responsibility and to maintain integrity, even in the midst of danger.

Cipher advocates using its power to unravel new horizons of knowledge. Their enthusiasm clashes with Aurora's caution, creating a friction between risk and prudence.

Shadow, contemplates the possible paths, aware of the implications of both decisions. Their concerns lie in the consequences of any choice, assessing the impact on the team and the outside world.

Ember, is torn between the desire to understand the artifact and the responsibility for its possible repercussions. Each discovery fuels their thirst for knowledge, but it also sets off alarm bells about the risks involved.

The pressure of the moment and the complexity of the options available to them pose a challenge that will test their deepest values, loyalties and convictions.The team is immersed in a struggle that goes beyond mere survival; It's about staying in control of something that can alter reality itself. Cipher,

Shadow, Aurora, and Ember, united by a common goal, face the harsh reality of having external and internal enemies. The philosophical differences between them intensify, sharpening internal fractures just when they need unity.

Cipher, always drawn to the artifact's limitless potential, finds himself at the epicenter of this storm. His bold vision clashes with the caution of Aurora, whose main goal is to protect and prevent power from falling into the wrong hands. Their arguments become sparks that ignite discussion about the way forward.

Shadow, detects enemy strategies and movements, aware of imminent danger. His skills are critical to navigating the chaos and keeping the team together, but his own doubts about the artifact's use add to the tensions.

Ember, dedicated to unraveling the mystery of the artifact, is torn between a fascination with its power and the responsibility to protect the world from its effects. Each discovery awakens ainternal dilemma, fueling their concerns about the consequences of their manipulation.

The confrontation with rival gangs not only threatens their physical safety, but also brings to light ideological differences that have been simmering.

In a showdown marked by tough decisions and the need for quick action, the team faces a challenge that will test their loyalties, values, and the strength bf their bond.

In the midst of the divided team, Aurora clings to her convictions, convinced that the responsibility to protect the artifact goes beyond her own group. Her steadfast determination to keep it hidden and away from any dangerous hands reflects her deep sense of responsibility and ethics.

Their argument is based on the fear of the catastrophic consequences that could be unleashed if the device fell into the wrong hands.

Every word of Aurora reflects her concern for the well-being of the world at large, and her proposal focuses on preserving stability and preventing the irreversible alteration of reality.

On the other hand, Cipher, driven by the prospect of employing the power of the artifact as a strategic tool, argues for a bolder and more ambitious position.For him, the artifact represents a unique opportunity to gain an advantage over his enemies, a way to tip the scales in his favor amid chaos and the struggle for control.

His vision, though risky, is imbued with a blind confidence in his ability to wield the power of the artifact and use it to his advantage. Cipher argues that his team can control him better than any other faction and that, in fact, his dominance could mean a more secure and controlled balance of power.

These opposing views lead to increasing tensions among team members.

The battle of ideas and values intensifies, fueling internal rifts and challenging group cohesion. In the midst of this storm of opinion, the decision about the fate of the artifact becomes an ethical dilemma that tests the convictions and loyalties of each member of the team.

Shadow, ever vigilant and observant, finds himself at a moral crossroads. Loyalty to his team faces uncertainty that plunges him into internal conflict. On the one hand, there's the strong bond he's built with his teammates, a loyalty rooted in years of collaboration and trust.The weight of these suspicions is compounded by external pressure from rival gangs. The constant threat of being stalked and attacked by unseen enemies keeps Shadow in a constant state of alert. The ethical dilemma of choosing between his loyalty to his team and the possibility that there are ulterior motives between them haunts him day and night.

Meanwhile, Ember finds himself at a similar crossroads. The ever-increasing understanding of the potential and danger of the artifact stirs up an internal struggle within it. On the one hand, the fascination and enthusiasm to discover the secrets of the artifact push him forward. Also, the responsibility of making sure the artifact doesn't wreak havoc and danger on the world haunts him.

The duality of his thinking is reflected in his actions and decisions. The excitement of discovering new capabilities clashes with concern about the potentially catastrophic consequences that could arise from their misuse. This internal struggle puts Ember at a moral crossroads, where the desire to know clashes with the responsibility to act prudently and ethically.

Both Shadow and Ember find themselves caught in a tangle of ethical and moral dilemmas, faced with decisions that could change the course of their lives and the fate of the artifact. Their conviction lies in protecting the world from the potential havoc that could ensue if the artifact's power falls into the wrong hands. His position, rooted in ethics and moral duty, clashes directly with Cipher's vision, for whom the artifact represents an opportunity for change and power. His strategic mind drives him to consider it as a tool to gain advantages over his enemies, even if it means taking greater risks.

The duality of these perspectives creates an abyss in the team, where trust and cohesion are threatened. The confrontation of ideals transcends the mere possession of the artifact; It becomes a clash of opposing philosophies, each backed by its own compelling arguments.

Aurora fervently advocates the preservation of the status quo, stability, and the protection of the known, while Cipher, with his bold and ambitious vision, embraces the notion of change and progress, even if that means stepping into dangerous and uncharted territory.

This clash of ideologies creates a rift in the team, splitting their forces in an internal struggle that goes beyond the mere desire to possess a coveted artifact. The plot is enriched with a moral and philosophical tension that adds depth to the narrative, raising ethical and existential questions that test the core values of each team member.

At the core of the team, the dilemma over the fate of the artifact becomes not only a confrontation over the possession of an object, but a war of ideologies that wounds the very foundations of their collaboration. The discussion room transforms into a battlefield where Aurora and Cipher's voices clash hard, each defending her vision ardently.

For Aurora, the responsibility to protect the world from the potential dangers that the artifact brings with it is an unquestionable principle. Their stance clings to stability, preservation of the known, and control to avoid any chaos.

Cipher insists on the need to use the device as a tool, a way to obtain strategic advantages that allow them to face the threats that loom over them. Its approach aligns with change, adaptability and seizing opportunities, even if this comes with incalculable risks.

Chapter 14

The Sacrifice

Getting to the heart of a crossroads always involves taking difficult paths, and sometimes it involves heartbreaking sacrifices. In this case, the team is plunged into a perplexing dilemma when one of its members is faced with an extremely dangerous situation. Faced with an imminent threat that stalks the group, one of them rises bravely ready to face the danger, knowing that the only way to protect others is to sacrifice themselves.

This act of bravery, while noble at its core, sets off an emotional whirlwind among the survivors. The first reaction is shock and awe at the boldness and courage of this team member. However, this brave action also stirs up additional tensions, an amalgam of emotions ranging from gratitude and acknowledgment to guilt and resentment.

The team is divided into a sea of mixed emotions. Courage and sacrifice are honored, but they also become a constant reminder of the price they have paid and the difficult choices they must face.

Some feel grateful for the sacrifice made on behalf of the group, while others struggle with feelings of guilt, wondering if they could have avoided such an outcome.

This heroic act profoundly alters the dynamics of the team. Internal tensions are intensifying, sparking heated debates about the meaning of sacrifice, the price of leadership, and the difficult choices that come in times of adversity. Bonds are strained, emotions are stirred and uncertainty hangs over the future of the team at a crucial moment.

In the heart of the storm, amid threats and latent dangers, the figure of Cipher stands as a beacon of courage and determination. With rival gangs intensifying their pursuit and the artifact at the center of the fray, Cipher finds himself in a harrowing dilemma. Faced with the imminence of a conflict that could endanger their comrades and the crucial goal they seek to protect, he makes a heartbreaking, but courageous, decision.

Fully aware of the importance of the artifact and the imminent risk it poses to the team, Cipher, with his sharp mind and unwavering mettle, decides to sacrifice his own safety. In an act of heroism and cunning, he becomes the distraction needed to divert attention from rival gangs, offering his comrades a chance to escape to safety. With steely determination, Cipher throws himself into the center of the

chaos, using his cunning and skills to create a curtain of distraction. His nimble mind and audacity become the shield that protects others, as he directly faces danger, averting eyes and holding back the threat to allow his comrades to move away from the battlefield.

This action is not only an act of selfless bravery, but also a symbol of Cipher's indomitable spirit. Their sacrifice, while painful, reflects their devotion to the team and their determination to protect the greater good.

However, this heroic decision triggers an amalgam of emotions within the group, from gratitude and respect to anguish and worry about Cipher's fate.

At the apex of desperation and urgency, Cipher stands as the team's pillar of courage and sacrifice. Certain that his act could mean a huge personal sacrifice, he decides

to take the lead in the fight against the rival gangs that harass the group. With a mixture of temperance and determination, he prepares to face the coming storm.

Defying imminent danger and aware of the possible consequences, Cipher becomes the force that will distract enemies. His agile, strategic mind and unwavering courage are his weapons in this matchup. With a meticulous plan in mind, he steps into the heart of the storm, knowing that his role is crucial to the survival of his companions.

Using his skills masterfully, Cipher orchestrates a choreography of distraction and cunning, manipulating circumstances to divert the attention of the pursuers.

As Cipher becomes the focus of enemy attention, his companions seize the opportunity to steer clear of danger. Their sacrifice is not only an act of heroism, but also a precise strategy that offers a crucial opportunity for the team's survival.

As he plays his role as a distraction, every second becomes a challenge for him, but his resolve remains unwavering, steadfast in his resolve to ensure the safety of others, no matter the personal cost.

Aurora, Shadow, and Ember are plunged into a whirlwind of mixed emotions after Cipher's heroic sacrifice. An amalgam of awe, gratitude, and grief weaves into their hearts as they reflect on the selfless act they witnessed. Cipher's bravery resonates deeply with them, but it also stirs up a sense of desolation and anguish.

Aurora feels a deep gratitude for Cipher's sacrificial act, but at the same time, a burden of guilt weighs on his shoulders. Doubts overwhelm her, questioning whether they could have found another alternative.

Shadow, faces an internal struggle. While he understands the necessity of Cipher's sacrifice, a sense of regret comes over him. He wonders if he could have intervened, if his skills could have offered a less drastic way out. Guilt nestles inside, fueling a feeling of helplessness and reflection on the decisions made.

Ember, feels a surge of admiration and sadness. He acknowledges Cipher's unwavering courage, but also faces his own questions about the consequences of his actions. A lingering uneasiness gripped him, questioning whether the research he was conducting could have revealed another solution, whether it could have contributed in some way to avoiding the culling.

The atmosphere among survivors is colored by this amalgam of emotions, creating a space where respect and gratitude are intermingled with guilt and regret. Cipher's sacrifice has not only marked their hearts, but has also left a legacy of questions and reflections on what could have been.

Emotions are woven into a whirlwind of grief and gratitude, shrouding the team in a haze of uncertainty and emotional vulnerability. Cipher's absence becomes an invisible but palpable weight that alters the group's dynamic.

The bonds between team members, once solid and reliable, are stretched to the limit. Not only did the loss of Cipher leave a tangible void in their team, but it also left an indelible mark on their hearts. The camaraderie that used to sustain them now feels fragile, like glass on the verge of shattering.

Chapter 15

The Point
of No Return

The members of the team are at a crucial point in their journey, caught in a juncture where possibilities seem to close around them. The urgency of the moment looms like a heavy slab on their shoulders, forcing them to carefully consider every move, every word, knowing that any decision could seal their fate.

The outlook they face is dizzying, with the paths forward blurred by uncertainty. Choices that were once presented as clear have now become blurred, each carrying with it a burden of risk and responsibility that weighs on their consciences.

The sense of no return manifests itself as a lingering echo in the air. Circumstances, shaped by unpredictable events, have brought them to a point where past decisions, ethical dilemmas, and internal relationships converge at a decisive crossroads.Aurora, feels pressured by the magnitude of the consequences of each choice. Her convictions are challenged, and the weight of leading the team at this crossroads pushes her to the limit of her ability.

Always alert to cues from the environment, Shadow finds himself at an emotional crossroads. Loyalty to his peers clashes with his need to protect his own integrity, plunging him into an internal struggle for decision-making.

At this crossroads, each team member faces their own dilemmas and fears, as time seems to speed up, forcing them to make a decision that will redefine their destiny and set the course of their odyssey. Cipher's absence hangs over the team like a shadow, leaving a void that seems impossible to fill. Each of the survivors carries the emotional weight of their sacrifice, as a constant reminder of the magnitude of the challenge they face. Their bravery becomes a beacon that illuminates the group's journey, but also an echo that resonates in their thoughts, reminding them of the fragility of their lives in this game of unknown forces.

The artifact's aura hovers over them, unleashing a mix of emotions. It is a treasure trove of untold potential, an opportunity to change the course of destiny, but also a Pandora's box fraught with unfathomable dangers. The duality of the artifact is revealed in every step they take, keeping their hopes and fears on tenterhooks, leading them into uncharted territory full of uncertainty and challenges.

Cipher's absence has created a rift in the group, a sense of vulnerability they hadn't experienced before. Strategies, once delineated with certainty, are now shrouded in doubts and deeper reflections. Decision-making becomes even more challenging, as Cipher's legacy resonates in every discussion, every planning, and every step they take.

The team is at an inflection point, facing the duality of possibilities and risks that the artifact represents. Cipher's legacy becomes a flame that stokes their resolve and, at the same time, a shadow that clouds their judgment, as they seek to unravel the enigma that now lies at the center of their lives.

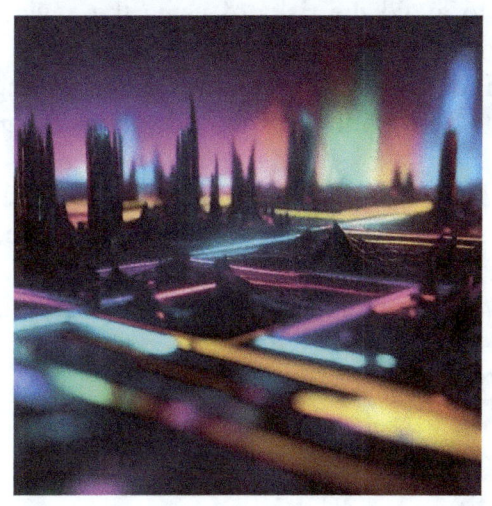

Before them unfolds a dark horizon full of uncertainty, marked by the urgency of an election that will change the course of history. The reality of being at a point of no return becomes inescapable, a truth that digs deep into their beings.

The room where they deliberate feels charged with tensions and dense silences. Each faces the magnitude of the decision they must make.

Aurora, struggles to find a balance between her desire to preserve stability and her fear of unleashing chaos if the artifact's power is mishandled. Shadow, in his quiet determination, contemplates the risks and possible consequences, weighing the cost of his actions and the implications of each route they may take. Ember, immersed in his obsession with deciphering the mysteries of the artifact, is faced with the dilemma of using his power for good or evil, while battling his own doubts and fears.

Each of them stands on a moral precipice, with their convictions and values colliding with the unforgiving realities before them. The future stretches out in front of them like a blank canvas, full of possibilities and dangers, and the choice they must make will reverberate throughout history, shaping the destiny of all those who will be affected by their determination.

Aurora, expressed her concern about the possible catastrophic consequences if the artifact fell into the wrong hands. Her words, imbued with caution, echoed through the room, outlining a future of chaos if the decision was wrong.

Shadow, with his calculated words, outlined the risks and the magnitude of the unknown they faced. Each of their arguments weighed the possibilities and warned of the dangers that could be unleashed if they took the wrong route. His tone, full of wisdom and caution, carried with it the seriousness of the moment.

Ember, wrapped up in his obsession with understanding the artifact, raised the revolutionary possibilities it offered. But his excitement conflicted with an inner anguish, for each advantage presented an equally significant risk. His voice, vibrating with excitement and fear in equal measure, reflected his inner dilemma.

The discussion became a whirlwind of divergent ideas, a dance of arguments leading to a dead end. No choice seemed to carry with it the certainty of a secure future, and the weight of responsibility weighed heavily on his shoulders. In the room, time seemed to stand still, while the pressure intensified with every argument presented, every inquisitive look, and every heavy silence.

In the dim light of the room, the silhouettes of Aurora, Shadow, and Ember were silhouetted against the gloomy backdrop. The weight of the impending decision was reflected in their countenances.

At every glance, there was a realization that they were at a pivotal point in history, where the line between greatness and disaster was thin, and any step could change the course of the world they knew. The halo of uncertainty that enveloped them gave a glimpse of the internal struggle that each one faced. Aurora, her eyes glowing with determination but also concern, weighed the possible ethical consequences of her actions.

In the stillness of the underground shelter, debate echoed among the team members. The central table, illuminated by dim flickering lights, served as a silent witness to the voices that were raised in discussion. Aurora, with her steady and serene gaze, vehemently expressed the importance of preserving the moral integrity and stability of the world. Her words, full of conviction, highlighted the imperative need to avoid the risks of using the device, focusing on protecting humanity from its destructive potential.

Shadow, argued for the need to consider the strategic possibilities offered by the device, underlining the usefulness it could have in neutralizing external threats and gaining a vital advantage in an increasingly unstable world.

Meanwhile, Ember, pondered the implications of his actions. Every word he uttered revealed his inner struggle, torn between the desire to explore the limits of the artifact and the responsibility to foresee the catastrophic consequences of misuse.

The final decision represented more than a mere verdict; It was a turning point in the history that was brewing between them.

Chapter 16

The Final
Revelation

The hours leading up to the revelation glided by with the slowness of expectation-laden moments. In the shelter, the atmosphere was imbued with an unsettling mixture of nervousness and anticipation. The members of the team gathered in the central room, surrounding Ember, whose grave and determined expression suggested the imminence of a crucial revelation.

Aurora, her gaze serene but full of expectation, waited patiently for the words that would come from Ember's lips. His face reflected the calm he was trying to convey, but his eyes betrayed the inner turmoil, yearning to understand the true purpose of the artifact so that he could make informed and responsible decisions.

Shadow, ever alert and observant, remained silent but with a palpable tension in his posture. His focused gesture denoted a concentrated expectation, yearning to understand the secrets the artifact held and the implications they could have for the team and the entire world.

Meanwhile, showed a hint of uneasiness that he seldom showed. His reserved and attentive demeanor betrayed the importance he attached to Ember's revelations, ready to assimilate the truths to come.

Ember, enveloped in an aura of seriousness and focus, prepared to unravel the enigmas surrounding the artifact. The heavy silence in the room was the premonition of a momentous moment, where Ember's words would be the key to unraveling the mystery that had kept the team on tenterhooks for so long.

Ember's words echoed through the room like echoes of a truth that challenged the foundations of human understanding. Each of his sentences was like a piece in the cosmic puzzle that had been hidden from everyone's view. His lips articulated cosmic truths that resonated in the souls of those present, a narrative that blurred the boundary between the known and the unknown.

As Ember revealed the essence of the artifact, each detail awakened a deeper understanding of the very nature of the universe. The words resonated with an energy that transcended the mundane, unveiling the mysteries hidden behind the object they had pursued so fervently.

Aurora, her eyes wide open, took in every word with a sense of wonder. Her mind expanded to embrace the vastness of Ember's revelations, her countenance reflecting an understanding that went beyond the words spoken.

Shadow, normally unfazed, was momentarily disarmed by the magnitude of what he heard. Each sentence resonated in his being, questioning the certainties he had held for so long, reframing his perception of reality.

Ember continued, each sentence a revelation that intertwined with the next, creating a tapestry of understanding that altered the perspective of the protagonists. The team was immersed in a state of reverence, taking in the magnitude of the truth that was being revealed to them.Ember's words echoed through the room like an echo of a newly discovered

universe. Each syllable was a doorway to the unknown, an enigma that slowly revealed itself as his lips articulated cosmic truths. In the silence that followed, the team members found themselves

immersed in a swirl of thoughts, as the truth gushed forth and challenged the structures of their understanding.

The purpose of the artifact, revealed by Ember, unleashed an avalanche of knowledge that seemed to have no bounds. What seemed like a simple object was now the key to understanding the deepest mysteries of the cosmos. Aurora, her eyes full of wonder, felt that each word broadened her horizons, reconfiguring her conceptual foundations.

Shadow, normally serene, was momentarily disoriented. Ember's revelations questioned the foundations of his reality, and each new concept blurred the boundaries of his understanding. The world as he knew it seemed to fragment before his eyes. Ember, with palpable serenity, continued to unravel the secrets of the artifact. Each new revelation was like a beacon illuminating an unknown cosmos, inviting the team into an ocean of understanding that stretched far beyond anything they had ever imagined.

The room fell into an overwhelming silence, each of the team caught up in the immensity of the revelation. Aurora's eyes reflected an amalgam of wonder and confusion, her mind struggling to embrace the breadth of new knowledge. The foundations of their reality were being dismantled, replaced by an understanding that defied logic and unleashed a swirl of inner questioning.

Shadow, always immersed in his own reflective darkness, found his tranquility challenged by Ember's words. The certainty of his world was fading, its boundaries blurred by the magnitude of the revelation. Every pillar of certainty on which he leaned tottered in the face of the vastness of the unknown.

The other members of the team were in a similar state of astonishment and bewilderment. Every word uttered by Ember opened a gap in his understanding of the world, allowing a mixture of fascination and fear of the unknown to flow. Each new piece of knowledge generated more questions than answers, plunging them into an ocean of uncertainty and wonder.

Ember, with a serenity in his expression, seemed to navigate the tumultuous waters of the new understanding with unshakable confidence. Every detail he revealed not only expanded the boundaries of knowledge, but also triggered deep reflection on the meaning of what they had discovered.

The silence became tangible in the room, only interrupted by the ragged breathing of the team members. Ember's revelation resonated in their minds, setting off a cascade of thoughts and emotions that challenged their understanding of the world. The artifact, once seen as a mere relic with unknown powers, now stood as a beacon illuminating the true nature of reality.

The foundations of his perception were slowly crumbling, as if Ember's every word pushed the boundaries of the known into an unknown abyss. For Aurora, who had always been the voice of reason, the revelation set off a firestorm of questions about the validity of everything she had believed. Shadow, with his observant spirit, struggled to reconcile the previous picture of reality with this new understanding. Ember's words echoed in his mind, eroding the solidity of his certainties.

Each member of the team was immersed in a vortex of internal reflections and dilemmas. The idea that reality itself could be shaped at will raised profound existential questions. Were they mere players on a vast stage controlled by forces they could not comprehend. The magnitude of what was revealed not only altered their perspectives, but also imposed on them the overwhelming responsibility of being guardians of a secret that could change the course of history.

Ember's revelation threw the team into an abyss of endless speculation and reflection. The realization that the artifact was not simply a powerful relic, but a key to a manipulable reality, shook the foundations of his understanding of the universe.

Aurora, with her analytical mind, plunged into a whirlpool of questions about the very nature of existence. Was reality an illusory construct? To what extent had it been shaped by outside forces?

For Shadow, the revelation represented a challenge to his perception of the truth. What did freedom really mean if reality itself could be altered at will? Their convictions about power and control faltered, leaving room for uncertainty.

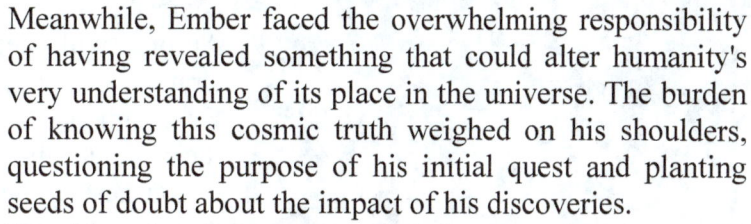

Meanwhile, Ember faced the overwhelming responsibility of having revealed something that could alter humanity's very understanding of its place in the universe. The burden of knowing this cosmic truth weighed on his shoulders, questioning the purpose of his initial quest and planting seeds of doubt about the impact of his discoveries.

The idea that forces beyond their comprehension could shape reality itself provoked a mixture of fascination and fear. The implications of this revelation brought them to the brink of an abyss, facing a reality far beyond what they had ever conceived.

Chapter 17

The Race
Against Time

The team, with racing hearts and minds overwhelmed by the magnitude of what has been revealed, plunges into a whirlwind of frenetic action. Urgency becomes his engine, knowing that time is an implacable enemy that runs against him.

Aurora, with her analytical mind, devises meticulous strategies for dealing with the impending consequences. Every minute counts in their race against catastrophe, and their determination to find a solution reflects the seriousness of the situation.

Always alert and agile, Shadow coordinates the team's movements precisely, looking for any signs of catastrophic change in the environment. Their acuity becomes an invaluable tool as they navigate the impending chaos.

Ember, consumed by the responsibility of having uncovered the truth, devotes himself to the search for a solution. Every formula, every equation, every theory is now a desperate attempt to amend the uncontrollable consequences of the artifact.

The mission is clear: to stabilize reality before it completely falls apart. The team's determination is steadfast, but every step toward a solution seems to be fraught with unknown obstacles. Anguish over the unknown and the hope of reversing the impending chaos drive them forward, even when adversity seems insurmountable.

Footsteps echoed on the convulsive pavement, an echo of despair amid the bustle of a blurred city. Aurora moved forward with determination, her sharp mind tracing lines of action on the chaotic canvas that the streets had become. Every move, every strategy outlined in her mind, carried the weight of responsibility for the fate of reality itself.

Shadow, moved deftly through the distorted alleys, his keen eye detecting any subtle change in the environment. The shadows danced, altering their form and presence, but their sharpness remained unscathed, watching for every sign of catastrophic change.

Ember, absorbed in his laboratory, immersed himself in experiments and calculations without pause. The passion for resolving the chaos that was unleashed was palpable in his concentrated face. Formulas and theories flowed in a desperate effort to find the counterweight that could stabilize the crumbling reality.The team, faced a distorted city. The buildings seemed to melt, the laws of nature

faltered, and uncertainty colored their every movement. Every step was a challenge, every moment a race against an ominous inevitability.

The mission was clear, but the chaos unleashed by the artifact had blurred even the clearest lines. In the midst of this challenge, their efforts were unified by a common conviction: to find a solution before the world completely fell apart.

Urgency filled the air, a constant throbbing that marked the rhythm of each action. Every attempt to restore normalcy was imbued with overwhelming responsibility.

The streets, once familiar, became a labyrinth of distortions and anomalies. The sky itself fluctuated in impossible hues,

while the buildings blurred before his eyes. Everything seemed to have been swept away by a capricious cosmic current.

Ember, experimented with matter itself. Complex formulas became the echo of a fight against time. Each equation solved was a small step toward normalcy, but the challenges were beyond human comprehension.

Aurora directed the action in the convulsed streets, looking for patterns in the chaos, trying to discern a logic where there seemed to be none. Her decisions were the anchor in the midst of the confusion, a compass for a team that was lost in a sea of distortions.

Shadow, always attentive to detail, moved among shifting shadows. His meticulous observations tried to detect the slightest clue that might lead to a solution, but the picture remained blurred.The team, was reeling under the weight of uncertainty and the magnitude of the task. Each attempt, though full of courage, seemed to be only a small step.

The walls of Ember's lab echoed with a frenzy of activity. Tubes and machines flashed and buzzed, reflecting the incessant work of the obsessed scientist. His eyes glowed with a mixture of determination and exhaustion, reflecting the magnitude of the challenge he faced.

Ancient manuscripts and advanced theories littered the tables, while Ember immersed himself in a maelstrom of equations and experiments. Every written formula, every configuration tested, was a step toward a deeper understanding of the very essence of the artifact. Ember's mind was an encyclopedia of possibilities, each idea a spark that could lead to the resolution of chaos.

Each discovery became a beacon of hope in the midst of darkness. However, the emotional burden of being the epicenter of the mission weighed heavily on his shoulders

The struggle to decipher the secrets of the artifact was a dance between genius and despair. Each attempt, though full of ingenuity and meticulousness, seemed to barely scratch the surface of a power that defied the limits of human knowledge.

Aurora's footsteps echoed in the empty corridors, as she immersed herself in the complexity of distorted reality. Her analytical mind traced invisible routes between bits of information, unraveling patterns in the seemingly chaotic. Every detail observed became one more piece in the puzzle they desperately needed to solve.

Shadow, with his keen insight, explored the margins of this altered reality. His heightened senses and ability to detect what escaped human sight became an invaluable resource. Every change in the disfigured landscape, every anomaly in the structure of the environment, was examined with surgical precision.The collaboration between Aurora and Shadow was a symphony of talent and determination.

They complemented their skills impressively, sharing knowledge and strategies in a dance of ingenuity and cooperation.

However, distorted reality did not easily give up its secrets. Each promising clue came with more questions, each breakthrough seeming to take them one step further away from the clarity they craved. The tension increased with each barrier encountered, reminding them of the magnitude of the challenge they faced and the urgency of finding a solution.

The hours seemed to melt like sand between the fingers of the team, whose concentration melted into a maelstrom of calculations and experiments. Ember, at the forefront of research, absorbed data, drew formulas, and conducted complex experiments with unparalleled intensity. Each outcome, each new revelation, was not only a step toward solution, but also a window into the magnitude of the challenge they faced.The lab became a melting pot of frenetic activity.Tension flowed like electricity in the air, mixed with the anxiety that accompanied every failed attempt and the relentless determination to find a way out. Words became whispers laden with uncertainty, gestures became more tense, and expressions reflected the gravity of the situation.

In every corner of the space dedicated to their research, the team immersed themselves in a frenzy of analysis, testing, and emerging solutions. The ticking of the clock became a steady drum marking the inexorably running out of time. Every minute felt like a step closer to the abyss, a constant pressure that pushed his abilities and limits to the extreme.

The urgency was palpable, permeating every decision made, every move made. The weight of responsibility was reflected in the faces of the team, aware that they were fighting not only for their survival, but for the fate of reality itself. Every effort was imbued with the burden of a goal that would not tolerate the slightest mistake.

Chapter 18

The Redemption

The weight of the past and the present consequences plunged them into an inner journey that challenged their deepest convictions. The wounds the artifact had inflicted were not only physical or tangible, but also emotional and spiritual, leaving indelible marks on their souls.

The team confronted their inner demons. Guilt, remorse, and frustration engulfed them, turning their hearts into a whirlwind of emotions. Each sought redemption, a way to make amends for the damage caused by the inadvertent manipulation of the artifact. They faced ethical and personal challenges that pushed them to the limit of their emotional and moral endurance.

Nights became moments of deep introspection, where the team searched their own souls for answers. The weight of past decisions became a burden impossible to ignore. Their faces reflected the internal struggle, their eyes charged with a tireless search for forgiveness, for redemption, and for finding a way to correct the course without falling prey to discouragement.

They were aware that the path of redemption would not be easy, but they were determined to walk it together, hoping to heal not only the external wounds, but also the internal scars.

In the stillness of the night, Aurora, Shadow, and Ember were immersed in a sea of turbulent thoughts. Their minds were the scene of an internal storm, where introspection became inevitable.

Guilt and remorse manifested themselves as dark, lingering shadows creeping into the corners of their consciousness. The initial spark of curiosity and ambition that led them to search for the artifact now turned into a flame of regret that burned their hearts. They recognized that their actions, motivated by a thirst for knowledge and the pursuit of power, had set off a chain of disastrous events.

Aurora, always firm in her convictions, found herself questioning her own leadership. The responsibility of guiding the team into this undertaking, now fraught with adverse consequences, weighed on her shoulders like a crushing burden. She wondered how she could have made different choices, looking for a path that would have avoided the current chaos.

Shadow, was besieged by the reality that his own ambitions had fueled this disaster. The memory of each strategy and strategic choice became an incessant echo of unanswered questions. Could he have foreseen the consequences? Would it have been possible to avoid the chaos that now engulfed their lives?

Ember, was faced with his own guilt. Every experiment, every advance in knowledge of the artifact, was now emotionally charged. The search for truth and understanding had become a thorny contradiction: the thirst for knowledge had led to an outcome he could not have foreseen.Together, they were plunged into an emotional journey in which they searched for answers.

The heavy chains of remorse and guilt were now the fuel for their effort. They recognized the magnitude of their role in the events that had brought the world to the brink and were determined to make amends.They vowed to do everything they could to repair the damage they had caused.

Aurora, became the voice of righteousness and moral guidance. She accepted her leadership role with humility, desperately looking for a way to make

amends for the decisions that had led the team down the wrong path. Their directives were clear: work together to undo the chaos they had unleashed.

Shadow, embarked on a mission of personal redemption. He used his sagacity to devise strategies to repair the collateral damage of his past decisions. Every move was filled with the determination to rectify the mistakes made, his sharp mind working tirelessly to find solutions.

Ember, dedicated every cell of his being to finding a solution.

Every experiment, every formula, was now a step toward reconciliation with the universe. Their quest for knowledge was tinged with a new motivation: to rectify the unexpected consequences of curiosity.

Together, fought with ironclad resolve, weaving strategies and working tirelessly to mitigate the consequences of their past actions. Each effort was a manifestation of their commitment to bringing stability and redemption to a world teetering on the brink of collapse.

Ember was immersed in a personal journey of self-discovery and deep reflection. Every step he took in his quest to restore harmony to the universe was a journey into his own morality, an internal struggle between the urge to right wrongs and the fear of making new ones. In his hands lay the knowledge that could shape the fate of the world or lead it into even greater chaos.

The responsibility weighed on his shoulders like an immeasurable burden.

He delved into the darkness of his own moral dilemmas, questioning how he should use this newfound power. His nights became a swirl of reflections, his mind wrestling with the duality between the desire to right the wrong and the fear of inflicting more.

Doubt was entangled in every experiment, in every attempt to manipulate the fabric of reality. The balance between good and evil became more diffuse as his mind navigated the turbulent waters of ethics and responsibility. He knew that the power to alter reality had to be wielded with caution and wisdom, but every potential solution came with unpredictable consequences.

Each advance in his research brought with it an inescapable duality: the hope of correcting past mistakes and the fear of unleashing new disasters. He was internally torn between the responsibility to do the right thing and the realization that every decision, every manipulation, could unleash new chaos.

Armed with the wisdom gained in adversity, Aurora and Shadow immersed themselves in building a new path. The priority was clear: to mitigate the consequences of the chaos unleashed by the artifact. Their inquisitive minds and unique abilities merged in creating ingenious strategies to stabilize the fractured reality.

heir commitment lay not only in correcting the mistakes made, but in creating safeguards for the future. They immersed themselves in an odyssey of ingenuity and collaboration, using their skills and

knowledge to weave a web of protection around the world, one that would prevent the mistakes of the past from being repeated in an uncertain future.

Redemption stood as a colossal challenge and, at the same time, as a path to transformation. The internal struggle between the desire to make amends and the burden of their previous actions became the engine that drove their commitment to the future.

As they progressed on this journey to redemption, they found themselves confronting their own limitations and weaknesses, but they also discovered the strength that lay in their collective resolve.

Chapter 19

The Last Sacrifice

The team, at the epicenter of a mission that transcended the physical, was in a state of relentless urgency. The pressure to restore reality and heal the fractures that had arisen in the very fabric of the world was crushing.

With each passing second, uncertainty grew, and with it, the awareness that the solution might require a harrowing price tag. A final decision, a momentous choice loomed on the horizon. An act of redemption, not without sacrifice, was seen as the only way to bring back the lost stability.

The team plunged into a whirlwind of internal debates, searching for an option that would balance the pressing need for reparation with the inevitable consequences of their choice. Each shouldered the weight of responsibility, facing the possibility that the road to restoration would require a final sacrifice.

The anguished looks and emotionally charged words reflected the palpable tension in the air.

In the midst of this maelstrom of doubts and mixed emotions, the team clung to hope, to the firm belief that even if the road to restoration was steep and full of sacrifice, their determination would prevail. They faced a dilemma that would test their humanity, but they were willing to face it courageously, with the conviction that redemption could emerge from even the darkest of times.

The team was at a crossroads, a pivotal point where decisions made could redeem their past mistakes or plunge the world into an uncertain fate. Each member carried the weight of their actions, a weight that felt like a slab on their shoulders, tearing at their hearts with every ethical dilemma that arose.

The very essence of his humanity was at stake. How far were they willing to go to right the wrongs of the past? Were they prepared to pay the price of redemption with unimaginable sacrifice?

The discussions became more and more intense and deeper. Each look reflected the emotional burden they carried, the weight of responsibility and the uncertainty of having to make decisions of such magnitude. Each team member's internal debate was a whirlwind of emotions, a constant struggle between what they knew was right and what the situation demanded.

Amid the darkness of their own doubts, they also clung to a glimmer of hope: the firm belief that even though the road to redemption was fraught with dilemmas and sacrifices, the restoration of the world was worth fighting for, even if it meant facing their deepest fears and making choices that would leave an indelible mark on their souls.

In the dim light of a room, the team members gathered, enveloped in a silence charged with tension and reflection. The uncertain glow of a faint light reflected on their worried faces, scarred by the gravity of the moment.

There was an idea floating in the air, a proposal that, though painful, loomed as the only possible one for the restoration of the world. The debate centered on the possibility of a final sacrifice, a heartbreaking act that could change the course of everything known.

Voices echoed through the room, their eyes revealed the emotional storm brewing in their souls, the weight of having to consider an option that challenged their most deeply held principles.

For Ember, the weight of newly acquired knowledge was intertwined with his search for solutions. He was aware that any decision would have unfathomable consequences. Aurora, with determination in her eyes, struggled with the responsibility to protect, but also with the dilemma of how far she was willing to go. Shadow, tormented by his own doubts and fears, was faced with the possibility of an uncertain future.

The decision they made would have an indelible impact, not only on themselves, but on everything they knew. It was a time when the boundaries between ethics and necessity were intertwined in a way that made them question the very foundations of their being. And so, in the midst of uncertainty, anguish and pain, they faced a dilemma that transcended the boundaries of the imaginable.

The weight of the moment filled the room, plunging the team members into a sepulchral silence. Their gazes, marked by seriousness and concern, were in a constant exchange, sharing the weight of a burden that neither wanted to carry. In the room steeped in uncertainty, the gravity of the situation enveloped every thought and feeling. The expressions reflected an amalgam of emotions: anxiety was intertwined with seriousness, sadness was drawn in his eyes, and anguish was reflected in every gesture.

They knew that the decision they were about to make would have unimaginable repercussions, that it would change the course of their lives and the world they knew forever.

Each wrestled with its own emotional baggage, torn between duty and desire, between morality and imperative necessity. Their eyes met, sharing an implicit understanding of the gravity of the moment. They had become the architects of destiny, facing a crossroads that demanded a difficult choice, one that would leave an indelible mark on their souls.

Amid the overwhelming stillness, the looks among the team members spoke louder than words, revealing sadness at the inevitability of what was to come and the emotional burden weighing on their hearts. It was a time when determination was mixed with resignation, where hope was intertwined with anguish, and where the uncertainty of the future was confronted by the responsibility of the present.

In the room, an overwhelming silence gripped the hearts of those present. The looks were eloquent, revealing the emotional whirlwind that was unleashed in their souls. Each member of the team was immersed in a maelstrom of thought, navigating between the possibilities and consequences of a final sacrifice. Emotions, as intense as they were contradictory, were entangled in their expressions. Determination, which drove their need to find a solution, was intertwined with fear of the unknown, weaving a web of uncertainty. The desire to redeem the wrongs of the past clashed violently with the anguish that accompanied the idea of the path to restoration.

In the depths of his eyes, there shone a desperate longing to resolve the crisis, an urgency to correct the deviant course of reality. However, there was also a trace of fear, a palpable fear of what the sacrifice could mean for each of them.

Each was at an emotional crossroads, torn between the weight of responsibility and the burden of the sacrifice that lay ahead. There was an air of resigned acceptance, though not without internal struggle. Their gazes reflected the amalgam of emotions, a kaleidoscope of intertwined longings, fears and desires at a crucial moment where the fate of the world and his own hung in the balance.

In the room, the discussion was entangled in intersecting arguments, reflecting the complexity of the situation. Each voice, charged with emotion, brought a different nuance to the conversation that became, at the same time, heartbreaking and hopeful.

The prospect of the final sacrifice, though painful and distressing, was seen by some as the only lifeline in a raging sea. It was the option that offered an opportunity, however uncertain, to restore the world to its original state, to undo the fractures and wounds that had torn reality itself.

Each perspective was imbued with the internal struggle between the need for redemption and the reluctance to make a decision that would irreversibly alter their lives. In the seesaw of opinions, intense emotions lurked: the hope of making amends for the past was met with fear of the consequences of an uncertain path to restoration.

Chapter 20

The New Reality

Their gazes were lost in the invisible horizon, burdened with the weight of the journey full of unexpected twists and revelations that had marked their lives indelibly.

Each reflected on the challenges overcome, the dangers faced, and the shocking truths discovered along the way. The artifact, now safe and contained, represented both a burden and a tangible reminder of all they had been through together. It was a testament to the strength of their union, but also a mirror that reflected the consequences of their choices and actions.In the shared silence, lessons learned through adversity resonated. The camaraderie forged in the midst of chaos, the difficult decisions made under pressure, and the responsibilities taken on for the greater good were woven into each other's thoughts. Past mistakes, now clear in hindsight, served as beacons to light the way to a more conscious and responsible future.

Between the lines of worry and determination, one could see the determination to move forward wisely, aware that each challenge overcome had left an indelible mark on their souls and shaped their worldview irreparably. It was a time of deep introspection, honest appraisal, and preparation for what would come next.

The shadows cast by the dim light slipped down the walls, creating an atmosphere enveloped in undisturbed silence. The team, gathered in that room, was immersed in a pause full of meaning, a moment full of reflection and contemplation. Their gazes reflected the emotional charge of a journey fraught with difficult choices and unexpected consequences.

Words were not necessary at the time; The silence spoke for itself. There was a mixture of understanding and remorse in their eyes, a deep understanding of the consequences of their past actions and a slight glimmer of remorse for the decisions that had brought them to this point.

Despite the weight of fatigue and the difficulties they faced, there was a glimmer of hope shining in their eyes. It was the spark of confidence, a flash of determination that clung to the possibility of a better tomorrow. Through the fatigue and sorrow, there was a thread of optimism, a tireless will to overcome adversity and learn from past mistakes.

In that shared silence, there was a kind of implicit pact between them. A quiet commitment to do the right thing, to mend what had been damaged, and to face the unknown with courage and resilience.

It was a time of collective introspection, where the past merged with the determination to build a brighter future, driven by the realization that lessons learned in the darkness of the past could light the way forward.

In the expectant silence that filled the room, Ember's voice rang out with a profound serenity.

"We are here, between the crossroads of what we know and what we have experienced," Ember began, his voice reverberating with a slow but steady cadence. "We have walked through uncharted territory, where reality itself seemed to question its very existence. And on this journey, we have come to understand the fragility of what we regard as the truth."

His words, laden with wisdom gained through the trials suffered, resounded in the heart of every individual present. "The responsibility that comes with

knowledge is immense. We have seen how our actions, driven by curiosity and ambition, can alter the very foundations of reality. But we've also learned that our mistakes can become the pillars of our wisdom."

Ember paused for a moment, allowing his words to settle in the air, before continuing. "Acknowledging our mistakes is the first step toward redemption. Accepting responsibility for our actions allows us to transform our failures into lessons, and these lessons into a compass for the future."

He paused, allowing his words to seep into the minds of those who heard him. "The road forward will not be easy. But we must look to the future with humility and determination. We must use our experiences for the common good, to protect and nurture what is truly valuable in this world, to make sure our actions have a positive and lasting impact."

His words resonated with a mixture of introspection and hope, appealing to the need to turn the darkness of the past into a light for tomorrow. In that room, in that instant, each individual was driven by a sense of shared purpose, inspired by Ember's words and the promise of a tomorrow guided by wisdom gained through adversity.

In the resounding silence that followed Ember's words, Aurora and Shadow exchanged knowing glances. Their silent gestures spoke of a connection beyond words, a mutual understanding rooted in shared challenges.

Aurora, with her determined gaze and serene expression, broke the silence. "Ember is right. Our journey has shown us the importance of acknowledging the fragility of our reality and the weight of our choices." Her words were calm but loaded with meaning, reflecting deep introspection.

Shadow nodded solemnly, adding in a reflective voice, "Ethics and morality are compasses on our journey. But how do we balance the pursuit of knowledge with the responsibility to preserve the stability of the world?" The question hung in the air, capturing the very essence of his dilemma.

The dialogue between the two became an exchange of ideas, a dance of perspectives where they explored the nuances of their own convictions. They spoke about the need to question, to seek answers, but also about the responsibility to protect what is valuable and precious in this world.

Aurora, with her focus on preservation, shared, "Curiosity is our driving force, but we must also recognize that with it comes a responsibility. Not just for us, but for everyone's well-being."

Shadow, who had always embraced exploration, added: "Exploration takes us to unknown places, but we must make sure that every step we take does not jeopardize the stability of everything around us."

As they continued the conversation, their voices resonated with a harmony of understanding and intertwined perspectives. At the time, every word was a step toward deeper understanding, an attempt to reconcile the desire for knowledge with the need to preserve what really mattered.

In the serene calm that enveloped the room, the team gathered in a circle, each member immersed in his or her own thoughts. It was Aurora who took the initiative, her eyes reflecting determination and hope, the desire to weave the collective strength they had cultivated.

"I'm sure we're stronger together," Aurora began, her voice echoing with conviction. "We have seen what the power of the artifact can unleash and we understand the responsibility that rests on us. We need to collaborate, trust and support each other more than ever."

Shadow nodded, his countenance reflective as he continued, "Each of us has unique abilities, and while our actions may seem insignificant in the grand scheme of things, we have learned that even the smallest actions can trigger meaningful change."

Ember, deep in thought, added: "Power is not just a tool; it's a responsibility. We must ensure that our actions are guided by a greater purpose, one that seeks to protect and preserve rather than control or dominate."

Each member of the team expressed their commitment to the noble cause of preventing the power of the artifact from falling into the wrong hands.

Each team member's eyes shone with renewed determination, committed to working together to preserve stability and protect the world from the forces that could unleash chaos.

In that circle of trust and commitment, they promised to collaborate, rely on their unique abilities, and use their acquired knowledge to ensure that the artifact's power was used for the greater good, thus preventing it from falling into the wrong hands.

In the dim light of the room, the words echoed like echoes of hope and determination. They had left behind the chaos unleashed by the artifact, but the uncertainty of tomorrow still persisted. Despite this, the team was immersed in a conversation full of optimism and resolve.

"Maybe this is a new beginning for all of us," Ember said, his eyes shining with a glimmer of hope. "We've learned so much on this journey, and now we have the opportunity to apply that knowledge to shape a better world."

The words echoed through the room, charged with a shared determination and an unwavering will to do good. Shadow reflected, "The future may be uncertain, but our intentions are not. We must take responsibility for our actions and turn them into a starting point for positive change."

Gestures and expressions revealed a consensus among them. In the midst of uncertainty, every word was imbued with the determination to build a future where power was exercised responsibly and ethics guided every step. United by a commitment to transform their experiences into catalysts for a safer and more ethical world, the team envisioned a horizon full of possibilities, full of opportunities to do good and learn from the lessons of the past.

www.ingramcontent.com/pod-product-compliance
Lightning Source LLC
Chambersburg PA
CBHW080852120626
46546CB00008B/2793